BEFORE IT BREAKS

The Seven Pillars of Trust Every Leader Must Build

Gearl Loden, Ph.D., MBA

Loden Leadership Press

For ***Monica,***

My wife, my partner, my friend, my greatest advocate, and my most steadfast supporter.

Without you, this journey would not be complete.

To the mentors and coaches who shaped me,

and to every leader who trusted me to walk alongside them,

your growth is the reason this book exists.

To Trey and Arthur,

I am so proud of the men you have become.

I cannot wait to see where your leadership journeys take you.

— Gearl Loden

Before It Breaks: The Seven Pillars of Trust Every Leader Must Build

Published by Loden Leadership Press

ISBN 979-8-9952177-1-8 (paperback)

ISBN 979-8-9952177-0-1 (hardback)

ISBN 979-8-9952177-2-5 (e-book)

ISBN 979-8-9952177-3-2 (audiobook)

The coaching stories and vignettes in this book are drawn from real leadership and coaching engagements. Names, roles, industries, and identifying details have been changed or combined to protect confidentiality. Any resemblance to specific individuals is coincidental.

The Loden Trust Framework™, Leadership Ledger™, 72-Hour Repair Protocol™, 90-Day Trust Build™, Trust-Protection Sequence™, Trust Audit™, The Capability-Commitment Diagnostic™, and Trust Signal Dashboard™ are trademarks of Loden Leadership and Consulting Group LLC.

Also available: Before It Breaks: The Complete Leadership Workbook — The Seven Pillars of TRUST Every Leader Must Build

First Edition

Praise for Before It Breaks

"The most important thing I know about lasting change—in a life, a team, or an organization—is that character under pressure isn't accidental. It's built. That's why Before It Breaks matters. The Coffee Bean is about choosing what you become when the water gets hot. Gearl Loden shows leaders how to build the trust infrastructure that lets a team hold its shape under heat. The Loden Trust Framework™ turns trust into seven behavioral disciplines—so your leadership doesn't fracture when it's tested. If you lead people, this book belongs on your desk."

— Damon West, bestselling co-author of The Coffee Bean

"'All in' is just talk if your team doesn't trust your leadership. Before It Breaks lays out seven disciplines that build real trust before pressure hits. Read it. Apply it. Then let the pressure reveal the foundation you built."

— Walter Bond, Mr. Breakthrough, Business Advisor

"HUMANeX has long emphasized that what leaders do drives culture and performance. Our research across over 20,000 teams—from school boards and cabinets to Olympic teams and West Point—highlights trust as the #1 variable in predicting great teams. Before It Breaks turns trust from a vague virtue into a practical leadership operating system—seven behavioral pillars with diagnostics and repair protocols leaders can run under pressure. Trust is the equivalent of oxygen for excellence."

— Brad Black, President and CEO, HUMANeX Ventures

"Lead for God's Sake! reminds us that leadership begins on the inside. Before It Breaks shows what must come next. Conviction alone does not sustain trust—structure does. These seven pillars translate purpose into disciplined, visible behavior so when pressure mounts, leaders don't drift and teams don't fracture. This is leadership built to hold."

— Todd Gongwer, Author of Lead for God's Sake!

"I work with coaches and leaders around the world, and the challenge is always the same: trust is essential, but rarely engineered. Before It Breaks turns trust into a buildable system. The seven pillars are the bedrock of human-centered coaching conversations and leadership decisions. The Loden Framework is a valuable tool for any leader and management team that desires to master leadership."

— Rashid Siddiqui, Co-Founder, International Coaching Institute

Contents

INTRODUCTION

Why Leaders Often Get Trust Wrong—And What to Do About It

Trust is not a leadership quality. It is infrastructure. Not metaphorically, operationally. When it holds, execution moves without friction, information travels without fear, and your best people stay and do the hardest work. When it breaks, everything that runs on top of it breaks with it: performance, communication, retention, and the speed of every decision that follows. Trust breaks faster than it builds. A single broken commitment can erase months of consistency. Most leaders know this from experience. Few manage it as a system.

Leaders are told to "build trust" the way they're told to "be strategic" or "create culture," as if repetition alone will make the concept actionable.

It doesn't.

Most leadership advice on trust falls into one of two traps. The first is inspirational: be authentic, be vulnerable, be present. These qualities matter, but they're insufficient. You can be all three and still run a low-trust organization. The second is transactional: deliver results, meet deadlines, hit targets. These are necessary, but inadequate. High-performing teams can still operate in fear.

What's missing is architecture.

Trust isn't a personality trait. It isn't a feeling. It isn't the residue of good intentions or the reward for consistent performance. Trust is infrastructure, the operating system that determines whether information flows clearly, whether problems surface early, whether execution moves without friction, and whether your best people remain.

This book is about the difference between running that system deliberately and running it by default.

I've spent more than two decades leading teams and coaching leaders across education, business, and executive leadership. In every sector, the patterns are consistent. The mechanics of trust don't shift when you move from a school district cabinet to a corporate boardroom to a founding team under pressure. The language changes. The stakes present differently. But the infrastructure that holds or breaks follows the same architecture, and the leaders who maintain it do so deliberately.

But before I explain the framework, I need to tell you how I learned it, from a season that cost me something.

The Season That Changed How I Lead

Part One: I Moved Too Fast

At the time, I was doing what leaders are rewarded for: seeing what others didn't yet see, making tough calls, and moving the organization toward something better.

The environment was demanding. Expectations were high. The work didn't pause because people were tired or because the calendar was full. There was always one more issue, one more stakeholder, one more decision that needed to be made and I was the one willing to own it.

And in that kind of pressure, speed feels like competence.

I had a decision in front of me that, from my seat, felt obvious. We had real constraints of time, budget, staffing, performance, and public expectations. We had a narrow window to act. I believed delay would cost more than action.

So, I accelerated a change.

Not with malice. Not with disregard. With conviction. I told myself I was protecting the organization from drift. I told myself the plan would be clearer once people saw the results. I told myself that if I explained the rationale well enough, alignment would follow.

Here's the part leaders seldom admit out loud: when you're capable and experienced, your confidence can become a kind of tunnel vision. You're not trying to control people. You're trying to protect momentum.

Momentum without trust is just force wearing a suit.

I implemented the change swiftly. And on paper, the decision was defensible.

But people weren't reading the paper. They were reading me.

They were reading the speed of the decision against how little input they had. They were reading the gap between what I said mattered, collaboration, transparency, and shared ownership, and what they experienced: a decision that arrived faster than the conversation did.

The resistance didn't come as pushback. It came as silence. Slower execution. Questions that sounded like compliance but carried doubt underneath. People didn't challenge the decision. They just stopped investing in it the way they had invested in decisions they helped shape.

That's the part no one warns you about. When trust starts leaking, it doesn't announce itself. It shows up as friction you can't name, work that should move but doesn't, conversations that should be honest but aren't, and alignment that sounds right but doesn't hold.

When trust is leaking, you must keep carrying the decision yourself. You're not just leading the work; you're managing the emotional reaction to the work, over and over again. It also changes you. It makes you less patient, less curious, and more convinced you need to push. You stop asking, "What am I missing?" and start asking, "Why won't they just execute?"

That shift can happen quietly in a leader's mind, long before it becomes visible.

By the time I realized what was happening, trust debt was already accumulating. Not because the decision was wrong, but because the trust architecture wasn't strong enough to survive the velocity.

Trust debt: the invisible accumulation of unaddressed decisions and signals that compound quietly until the system fails.

Looking back, I can name exactly what broke.

Clarity leaked first. People didn't fully understand what was changing, why it mattered, what would not change, and what success would look like. In uncertainty, the human mind fills blanks with fear. People don't need every detail. They need enough clarity to stop guessing.

Consistency leaked next. The standards around decision-making weren't predictable. People couldn't tell what inputs mattered, how trade-offs were being made, or whether exceptions were becoming policy. Without consistency, leaders become hard to read; and people don't trust what they can't read.

Care became invisible. Not because I didn't care, but because care wasn't structurally present in the process. Some experienced the speed as disregard. They didn't feel protected by the change. Leaders can care deeply and still create environments where people don't feel cared about.

Intent doesn't travel on its own.
Infrastructure is its superhighway.

I didn't know yet that I was watching trust break before it "broke." The fracture was happening privately, long before it became public.

Which is why the second moment matters.

Part Two: When Trust Debt Went Public

The governance meeting wasn't when trust broke. It was simply the moment trust debt became visible.

High-stakes settings compress what has been accumulating in private and put it under a spotlight. The room wasn't hostile; it was cautious. And caution in a governance setting is one of the clearest trust signals a leader can receive. It means people are managing risk instead of engaging with possibility.

The questions weren't adversarial. They were careful. Careful questions from people who should have felt confident enough to be direct. That gap, between the directness I expected and the caution I experienced, told me more than the words themselves.

Something was off, and it wasn't the room. It was the residue of how I had been leading in the months before.

At that moment, I had a choice. I could explain. I could present the data, walk through the rationale, defend the process, and attempt to win the room through logic.

Or I could do something harder.

I could name what was true.

Leaders don't just manage outcomes. We manage confidence. And confidence isn't maintained with logic alone. It's maintained with predictability, transparency, and the visible discipline of how decisions get made.

So I stopped trying to win the room. I stopped trying to convince them I was right.

I acknowledged that my process had created distance. I owned the gap between what I believed I was doing and what it looked like from the outside. I clarified what I should have clarified earlier: what was known, what wasn't, what constraints were real, what options were on the table, and where governance input genuinely mattered.

Then I did something leaders often avoid because it feels like surrender. I set a standard for the future, out loud. Not a vague promise. A discipline. I explained how, moving forward, decisions like this would be surfaced earlier. I explained the communication cadence I would hold, how and when information would be shared, and how we would ensure the room never had to ask again, "Why didn't we hear sooner?"

I stopped trying to repair trust with reassurance and started rebuilding it with repeatable behavior.

That meeting didn't "teach me to communicate better." That's too small.

It forced a deeper shift. From relying on personal credibility to building institutional credibility. From assuming trust to maintaining it. From leading through force of personality to leading through force of architecture.

What That Season Built

That season changed how I think about leadership. I used to believe trust was primarily relational, built through goodwill, authenticity, and strong intentions. Now I see trust as operational. Not emotional. Not sentimental. Operational. Trust is what allows leaders to move fast without leaving people behind. It's what allows teams to stay aligned under pressure. It's what prevents a single decision from becoming a referendum on your character.

The reason many leaders struggle with trust isn't that they're untrustworthy. It's because they don't run trust as a discipline.

Before I act on any high-stakes decision, I slow down long enough to name the real risk. I think about what people will hear as I decide what to say. I identify who needs to understand the decision before it's announced, not after. I build clarity into the process early, because the gap between what I know and what others know is where trust leaks fastest. I use consistency in messaging as a way to develop clarity. I make care visible through structures we put in place to support the people I lead.

The failures I described above didn't just change how I lead. They gave me what I couldn't find on any shelf: a reason to build what you're about to read.

What This Book Is—And What It Isn't

This is not a motivational book about becoming a better person so people will trust you more.

This is a book about building systems that produce trust, regardless of your personality, your industry, or the pressure you are under.

The Loden Trust Framework™ is built on seven pillars: Character, Consistency, Communication, Competence, Care, Clarity, and Courage. Each pillar represents a behavioral discipline, a set of decisions leaders make or fail to make, that determines whether trust strengthens or erodes over time.

These pillars are not values to which one aspires. They are load-bearing structures. Remove one, and the system weakens. Neglect several, and the system collapses, often in the exact moment you need it most.

The book is organized into four parts.

Part One: Foundation explains how trust functions as an operating system and how it breaks before most leaders notice. It includes a Trust Audit™ to help you diagnose where your trust system is strong and where it's already fracturing.

Part Two: The Seven Pillars walks through each pillar in depth, the behaviors that build it, the patterns that break it, the leadership decisions that test it, and real coaching moments that show what each pillar looks like under pressure.

Part Three: Running the System introduces the operational tools, the Leadership Ledger™ for tracking how decisions land over time, the Trust Signal Dashboard™ for reading drift early and the 72-Hour Repair Protocol™ for fast, targeted trust repair when fractures occur.

Part Four: When Trust Breaks addresses the hardest questions: why some trust failures actually increase credibility, what leaders leave behind when they're no longer in the room, and how to rebuild trust from the ground up in 90 days.

Every chapter is designed to be studied, not just read. The appendices include conversation scripts, advanced diagnostics, a quarterly scorecard, and a facilitation guide you can use with your leadership team.

What Makes This Framework Different

Most trust frameworks describe trustworthy leadership. This one diagnoses it. They identify qualities, behaviors, and relational disciplines that strengthen credibility over time. That work matters. What this framework is built to do is different. The Loden Trust Framework™ is not primarily a portrait of trustworthy leadership. It is a diagnostic operating system designed to help leaders determine which pillar is under strain, what signals appear first, and how to repair trust before drift becomes fracture. You do not need another list of admirable qualities. You need a system that works under pressure. This is that system.

A Note Before We Begin

I wrote this book for the CEO, senior leader, superintendent, founder, or executive whose decisions shape what others experience as their day, who senses that something isn't landing the way they intend. It is for those who work harder than most people around them and still feel the weight of uncertainty in the system.

I wrote it because I was that leader. And because the shift from leading on instinct to leading on infrastructure changed everything, not just for the organizations I served but for the kind of leader I became.

"Trust rarely breaks all at once. It weakens first where leaders stop tending to it."

This book is about attending to trust. Deliberately. Systematically. Starting now.

Start with Part One. Move deliberately. Apply what you learn.

How to Use This Book

This book was designed to be more than a read. It was designed to be a system you run.

A note about the coaching stories throughout this book: every vignette is drawn from real leadership and coaching engagements across education leadership, executive teams, and organizational change work. Names, roles, industries, and identifying details have been changed or combined to protect confidentiality. The patterns are real. The leadership dynamics are real. This note applies to every story in the book. You will not see it again.

Move through it sequentially, from Part One through Part Four, building the Loden Trust Framework™ layer by layer. Or go directly to the section most relevant to your situation right now, the pillar that's leaking, the relationship that's strained, the recovery that needs a map. Either path works.

At the end of most chapters, you'll find a System Check, a set of questions designed to connect the chapter to your current leadership reality. They are not rhetorical. Engage them as a mirror before you use them as a map. The leaders who get the most from this book are the ones who stop at those questions, sit with the discomfort, and answer honestly before moving on.

The appendices are working tools: conversation scripts, diagnostics, repair playbooks, and the Trust Scorecard™. Return to them often. Leaders may find they use the appendices as much or more than the chapters.

A companion workbook is also available for those who want to go deeper. It provides structured space to work through each pillar, complete the diagnostics, and apply the framework to your current leadership reality.

Read with a pen in hand. Write in the margins. Then go lead differently.

The architecture is in your hands. Lead deliberately.

— Gearl Loden

PART ONE—THE FOUNDATION

CHAPTER 1: TRUST AS AN OPERATING SYSTEM

"Every leader runs a trust system. The only question is whether they run it deliberately or by default." — *Gearl Loden*

The Introduction showed what happens when that system runs by default. This chapter explains how the system works, so you can run it deliberately.

Leaders often think about trust the wrong way.

They treat it as a relationship variable, something built through authenticity, rapport, or shared experience. They believe trust grows when people like each other, when communication is open, and when teams bond over shared challenges.

None of that is wrong, but it's incomplete.

Because trust is not primarily a relationship outcome.

Trust Is Infrastructure

It's the operating system that determines whether information flows honestly or gets filtered on the way up. It governs whether people raise problems early or hold them until they become crises. It shapes whether execution moves quickly or stalls in endless clarification loops; whether feedback lands as honest or performative; and whether standards hold under pressure or quietly erode when no one is watching.

Like any operating system, trust governs normal operations: it sets the rules and determines what's possible. And like any infrastructure, it can be run well or run poorly, but it can't be avoided.

Trust Is Not Optional

Every leader runs a trust system.

The only question is whether they run it deliberately or by default.

Leaders who run trust by default react to trust problems after they surface. They can't name which behaviors build trust and which erode it. They confuse trust with popularity or likability, and they treat trust as something that "just happens" when culture is good. When trust breaks, they're blindsided, not because the signals weren't there, but because they never learned to read them.

Leaders who run trust deliberately track trust signals before problems surface. They know which specific behaviors strengthen which pillars. They diagnose fractures early and repair them quickly. They separate trust from affection because you can trust someone you don't particularly like, and you can like someone you'd never trust with a consequential decision. Most importantly, they treat trust as a system they're responsible for maintaining, not an outcome they hope to attain.

What an Operating System Does

An operating system (OS) has three jobs.

Job 1: Set the rules for normal operation. An OS determines how programs run, how resources are allocated, and how processes interact. It creates predictability.

Trust does the same thing. It determines how decisions get made, how communication flows, how mistakes are handled, how feedback is given, and how conflicts are resolved. When trust is strong, these processes run cleanly. When trust is broken, processes become friction.

Job 2: Govern behavior under pressure. Operating systems are tested under load. When memory is constrained, when processing power is maxed, and when multiple programs compete for resources, the OS determines what happens.

Trust works the same way. It's tested when budgets get cut, when deadlines compress, when mistakes go public, when priorities conflict, and when leaders are stretched thin. Strong trust systems are under pressure. Weak trust systems collapse, and they collapse fastest in precisely the moment you need them most.

Job 3: Enable or constrain what's possible. A good OS makes complex tasks simple. A bad OS makes simple tasks impossible.

Trust works identically. High-trust environments enable speed, autonomy, honest feedback, creative risk-taking, and fast recovery from mistakes. Low-trust environments require excessive oversight, documentation, meetings, approvals, and political navigation. The gap between these two environments isn't the cultural atmosphere. It's operational capacity.

Trust determines the ceiling of what your team can accomplish.

The Seven Load-Bearing Pillars

Trust doesn't break evenly. It fractures along predictable lines.

This framework identifies seven pillars that bear the load.

Character: Do your values hold when there is pressure?

Consistency: Do people experience predictable leadership behavior, especially under high-stakes situations?

Communication: Do people understand the "why" behind decisions before those decisions surprise them?

Competence: Do systems work reliably, or does execution depend on heroics?

Care: Are you protecting people's capacity or just their feelings?

Clarity: Does truth move faster than rumor?

Courage: Do you address what needs addressing or delay until forced?

These pillars are not personality traits. They are behaviors leaders demonstrate, and systems leaders build.

One distinction worth naming now: Character governs what you stand for when tested. Courage governs when you act on what needs addressing. Both are tested under pressure. Both are required. But they fail differently, and they're repaired differently. The chapters ahead will make that clear.

Why Pillars, Not Principles

The pillar metaphor is intentional.

Pillars bear weight. Remove one, and the structure weakens. Remove several, and the structure collapses.

Leaders often focus on one pillar while neglecting others. They communicate well but avoid hard conversations: strong Communication, weak Courage. They care deeply but let standards slide strong Care, weak Character. They set clear direction but go silent when the conversation gets hard: strong Clarity, weak Courage. Every combination is possible. Trust requires all seven pillars to function, not just the ones that come naturally.

Not perfection in all seven, but functionality.

A structure can tolerate minor cracks in a pillar. It can't tolerate missing pillars.

How Trust Systems Fail

Most trust failures follow a predictable pattern. It starts with pressure: budget cuts, tight deadlines, board scrutiny, organizational change, or personal stress. The source varies. The sequence doesn't.

Under pressure, the leader's behavior shifts. They stop explaining decisions, and Communication weakens. They micromanage or check work they used to trust, and Consistency breaks. They delay hard conversations, and Courage erodes. They add work without removing anything, and Care fractures. They stop naming what success looks like, and Clarity disappears. They cut corners on standards they used to model, and Character quietly erodes. They stop demonstrating that they know what they're doing, and Competence, or at least the team's confidence in it, begins to fade.

None of these shifts feels dramatic at the moment. They feel like reasonable adaptations to difficult circumstances.

But the team notices before the leader does.

The leader doesn't notice because their intent hasn't changed. They think *I'm managing a crisis. They understand.* The team experiences something entirely different: *Standards are changing. We don't know what to expect anymore.*

Then trust leaks quietly. People stop volunteering information. They ask permission for things they used to own. They document conversations to protect themselves. They stop bringing problems early. None of this happens loudly. It happens in the space between what people used to do freely and what they now do cautiously.

When the leader finally notices, they often misdiagnose. The symptoms are visible: execution is slow, communication feels filtered, morale is low, and people seem disengaged. But the leader doesn't connect those symptoms to their own behavior shift. The real diagnosis: the trust system broke under load, and the leader didn't notice.

The Asymmetry Problem

Trust breaks invisibly because of asymmetry.

Leaders experience their intent. Teams experience observable behavior.

This is why leaders are often blindsided. The leader thinks, "I've been working harder than ever. Why is the team frustrated?" The team thinks, "Leadership is erratic. We don't know what they want anymore."

Both perspectives are true. Only one is operational.

Intent is invisible.
Behavior is visible.

Trust is built or broken on what people see and hear, not what leaders intend.

Why Most Trust Advice Fails

Most trust advice fails because it addresses symptoms, not structure.

"Communicate more openly" doesn't specify what to communicate, when, or how. "Be more consistent" doesn't identify which behaviors are inconsistent. "Show you care" doesn't distinguish between care that protects feelings and care that protects capacity. The advice sounds right, yet it doesn't work.

This book gives four things most leaders never get: diagnostics to identify which pillar is failing, signals to catch trust drift before it becomes a crisis, repair protocols to restore trust after fractures, and operational behaviors that strengthen each pillar. *Not inspiration. Infrastructure.*

What's Next

The next chapter explains how trust breaks before you notice and how to catch it early. We'll then walk through each of the seven pillars in depth.

But first, a critical question:

Are you managing trust deliberately or by default?

Most leaders don't know. They've never diagnosed their trust system. They've never identified which pillars are strong and which are fragile.

If you don't know where trust is leaking, you can't repair it.

Chapter 2 provides the diagnosis.

Before we move to Chapter 2, one concept worth carrying into everything that follows: Every high-stakes decision creates two tracks of work. The first track is the decision itself: the strategy, the data, the action. Most leaders are very good at this track. The second track is the trust architecture around the decision: how it lands, what meaning people attach to the process, and whether the system stays steady or starts leaking. Most leaders skip this track entirely or address it after damage is already done. As you move through the Seven Pillars, be sure to keep the second track in mind. You will see it operating in every chapter.

Your System Check:

- *Before we move forward, one question worth sitting with:*
- *Think about the last time trust broke on your team.*
- *Which came first? A change in your behavior under pressure, or a change in your team's behavior?*

If you answered, "the team's behavior," look again. You missed the moment your own behavior shifted, but your team didn't.

- *Now name one behavior you will recalibrate this week before your team has to notice it for you.*

CHAPTER 2: TRUST BREAKS BEFORE YOU KNOW IT

"Trust doesn't announce itself when it's breaking. By the time most leaders notice, the damage is already serious."

—Gearl Loden

Trust doesn't announce itself when it breaks.

There's no alarm. No flashing dashboard. No moment when someone says, "We don't trust you anymore."

Instead, trust erodes quietly, through small behavior shifts, micro-decisions, and unspoken conclusions.

By the time leaders notice trust is broken, the damage is often serious and the repair costly.

This chapter explains why trust breaks invisibly, the signals that reveal trust drift before crisis hits, how to diagnose which pillar is fracturing, and why the slow leak is one of the most dangerous kinds of failure.

The Slow Leak Problem

Most leaders assume trust breaks suddenly, through a major mistake, a public failure, or a betrayed confidence.

Sometimes it does.

But more often, trust breaks slowly. Through patterns.

A leader makes an exception to a standard "just this once." Then again. Then again. Eventually, the team concludes standards are negotiable.

A leader withholds information to "avoid unnecessary worry." Then does it again. And again. Eventually, the team concludes, "We're not trusted with the truth."

A leader delays a hard conversation to "wait for the right time." Weeks pass. Months pass. Eventually, the team concludes leadership avoids accountability.

None of these moments feel like trust-breaking events when they happen. They feel like reasonable judgment calls.

But they compound.

Why Leaders Miss the Signals

Trust breaks invisibly for two reasons:

Reason 1: Leaders experience intent. Teams experience outcomes.

What the leader thinks: "I'm bending the standard because the situation is unique. The team will understand the exception."

What the team sees: "The standard changed without explanation. We don't know what's expected anymore."

What the leader thinks: "I'm delaying this conversation until I have all the facts. I don't want to jump to conclusions."

What the team sees: "Leadership knows there's a problem and isn't addressing it. Either they don't care, or they're avoiding it."

The leader's intent is invisible. The team only sees behavior.

Reason 2: Trust information flows asymmetrically.

Bad news travels up slowly, or not at all.

When trust starts eroding, the first people to notice are the people experiencing it. They almost never tell the leader.

They assume the leader already knows. They fear appearing negative or disloyal. They may have tested the waters before and been dismissed. They're waiting to see if it's a pattern or a one-time thing.

These factors leave the leader operating without feedback. The leader doesn't realize trust is fracturing because no one is telling them.

By the time the signal is loud enough to reach the leader, trust isn't just cracked, it's shattered.

The Eight Signals of Trust Drift

Trust drift reveals itself through specific, observable signals.

Leaders who learn to read these signals catch trust fractures early, when repair is still simple.

Signal 1: People start asking permission for things they used to decide independently.

What it means: They're no longer confident they understand the decision framework.

Which pillar is breaking: Consistency or Clarity (or both)

What to ask yourself: Have I changed expectations without explaining why? Are the decisions I make predictable, or are people guessing?

Signal 2: Questions decrease in meetings.

What it means: People have stopped believing their questions will be answered honestly, or they've concluded that asking questions is risky.

Which pillar is breaking: Clarity, Communication, or Courage

What to ask yourself: Have I shut down questions? Do people feel safe raising concerns? Am I explaining the "why" behind decisions?

Signal 3: Execution slows, even on straightforward tasks.

What it means: People are documenting, double-checking, and seeking confirmation because they don't trust that the system will protect them if something goes wrong.

Which pillar is breaking: Care, Competence, or Consistency

What to ask yourself: Do people trust the system, or are they building workarounds to protect themselves?

Signal 4: High performers stop volunteering for new projects.

What it means: They're burned out, disengaged, or no longer confident that effort will be recognized or that the organization will protect their capacity.

Which pillar is breaking: Care or Character

What to ask yourself: Am I rewarding high performance with more work? Are my best people sustainable, or am I breaking them?

Signal 5: Rumors spread faster than official communication.

What it means: Leadership is not communicating frequently enough or in ways that connect with their team, or people don't trust that they'll get the truth from leadership, so they're seeking it elsewhere.

Which pillar is breaking: Communication or Clarity

What to ask yourself: Am I withholding information? Is my communication too slow or too vague? Am I communicating in the way that best suits my team or myself?

Signal 6: People stop bringing you problems early.

What it means: They've concluded that raising problems early is either risky or ineffective.

Which pillar is breaking: Consistency, Clarity, or Courage

What to ask yourself: Do I shoot the messenger? Do I delay addressing issues people bring me? Do people know what to expect from me, or do they brace for a different leader depending on the day?

Signal 7: Conversations happen "around" you instead of "with" you.

What it means: People have stopped believing that direct communication with you will be productive.

Which pillar is breaking: Character, Communication, or Courage

What to ask yourself: Have I made it unsafe to bring me hard truths? Do people trust my response when challenged?

Signal 8: Small mistakes trigger disproportionate emotional reactions.

What it means: Trust reserves are depleted. When trust is strong, small mistakes are absorbed easily. When trust is low, every mistake feels like confirmation of systemic failure.

Which pillar is breaking: Multiple pillars (this is a late-stage symptom)

What to ask yourself: Which pillar broke first? Where did the erosion start?

The Trust Audit™: A Diagnostic Tool

Note: In this audit, you are counting warning signs. The fewer you identify, the stronger the pillar.

This is not a psychometric instrument. It's a diagnostic discipline, a structured way to demand honesty about what your team is experiencing. The value is in the patterns the questions surface. It works for individual leaders; it works better when a leadership team completes it independently and compares scores. The gaps between how you score yourself and how others score you are where the real diagnosis lives.

How to use it: For each pillar, assess three dimensions:

- Your behavior as a leader, not your intentions, your actions
- Signals you're seeing from your team, what they're doing, not what they're saying
- System evidence, the observable patterns that exist, whether you acknowledge them or not

For each question, answer "Yes" or "No." If your honest answer is "sometimes," "I'm not sure," or "I don't know," count it as Yes. Answer based on what your team would say, not what you intend. Uncertainty is a signal. The most honest version of this audit is the one someone else completes about you.

This audit is most powerful when it becomes a recurring discipline, not a one-time exercise. Retake it quarterly. Trust doesn't hold still, and neither should your awareness of it. When you track scores across quarters, you stop reacting to trust problems and start reading them in advance. A pillar that scored a 3 in January and a 5 by April is telling you something no survey or exit interview will say out loud. Build this into your leadership rhythm. The leaders who audit trust consistently are almost never the ones scrambling to repair it.

Note: The Trust Audit™ can be: Used as a self-reflection tool, for 360-degree feedback, and as a team activity.

Answer honestly. Score each pillar:

0–2 warning signs = Pillar is a cornerstone for trust

3–4 warning signs = Pillar is strong

5–6 warning signs = Pillar is fragile

7+ warning signs = Pillar is broken

Pillar: Character

Leader's Behavior Assessment:

- When values and convenience conflict, convenience wins?
- Have I delayed decisions that require personal cost?
- Have I made exceptions for myself that I wouldn't allow others?

Team Signal Assessment:

- Am I modeling what I'm asking of others?
- Does cynicism increase when I talk about values?
- Would my team say that my words don't match my actions?

System Evidence Assessment:

- Do standards shift based on who's involved?
- Are values stated but not enforced?
- Do people question my motives more than my methods?

Character Score: ___ warning signs

Pillar: Consistency

Leader Behavior Assessment:

- Would my team say I respond to similar situations inconsistently?
- Have I changed expectations without explaining why in the last 90 days?
- Would my team say I apply standards differently depending on who is involved?

Team Signal Assessment:

- Are people asking permission for things they used to decide independently?
- Have candid conversations been replaced with careful ones?
- Are people telling me what I want to hear instead of what I need to know?

System Evidence Assessment:

- Are decisions escalated to me that shouldn't be?
- Does execution vary widely depending on who's managing it?
- Do people wait for direction on things that should already have clear expectations?

Consistency Score: ___ warning signs

Pillar: Communication

Leader Behavior Assessment:

- Would my team say that I don't explain the "why" before announcing decisions?
- Do I wait to be asked before I communicate?
- Am I withholding information because "the timing isn't right"?

Team Signal Assessment:

- Do people say "I wish I'd known sooner"?
- Do rumors spread faster than official communication?
- Are people surprised when decisions are announced?

System Evidence Assessment:

- Are decisions walked back frequently after implementation?
- Do people operate on outdated information?
- Is execution delayed because "we didn't understand what you meant"?

Communication Score: ___ warning signs

Pillar: Competence

Leader Behavior Assessment:

- Do results depend on me personally more than our systems?
- Am I promoting people faster than they're developing?
- Do I double-check work that my team should own?

Team Signal Assessment:

- Are people over-documenting to protect themselves?
- Are high performers burning out covering for low performers?
- Are people asking "Did I do this right?" more than "What should we do next?"

System Evidence Assessment:

- Do outcomes vary significantly based on who's executing?
- Do failures repeat without correction?
- Are people waiting for me to solve problems they should own?

Competence Score: ___ warning signs

Pillar: Care

Leader Behavior Assessment:

- Am I prioritizing people's comfort over their actual capacity?
- Have I failed to remove unnecessary work in the last 90 days?
- Am I lowering standards instead of holding them in order to appear kind?

Team Signal Assessment:

- Are high performers disengaging or leaving?
- Is burnout normalized?
- Do people say "yes" but deliver "no"?

System Evidence Assessment:

- Is the workload increasing without anything being removed?
- Are people working late regularly?
- Is resentment building between high and low performers?

Care Score: ___ warning signs

Pillar: Clarity

Leader Behavior Assessment:

- Would my team struggle to repeat back what success looks like after our conversations?
- Do I speak in generalities when specifics are needed?
- Am I avoiding naming what's actually wrong?

Team Signal Assessment:

- Do people ask "What do you mean?" frequently?

- Does execution not match intent?
- Are teams creating their own interpretations of my direction?

System Evidence Assessment:

- Are decisions relitigated after they're made?
- Do people execute differently despite hearing the same message?
- Is confusion treated as a people problem, not a clarity problem?

Clarity Score: ___ warning signs

Pillar: Courage

Leader Behavior Assessment:

- Have I let hard conversations go unaddressed for more than 72 hours?
- Am I avoiding decisions because they're uncomfortable?
- Have I sent the message that standards are negotiable when pressure rises?

Team Signal Assessment:

- Do people say, "Everyone knows this isn't working?"
- Do problems persist despite awareness?
- Is my team having conversations without me?

System Evidence Assessment:

- Do issues surface late, not early?
- Are performance problems going unaddressed?
- Have people stopped bringing me bad news?

Courage Score: ___ warning signs

Interpreting Your Audit

If all pillars scored 0–2: Trust is operating at a high level, and your team feels it. Decisions move without unnecessary friction. People bring you problems early because they believe you'll handle them well. Don't mistake this for finished work. Trust at this level is maintained through daily discipline, not autopilot.

If most pillars scored 3–4: Trust is present and developing, but it hasn't hardened into infrastructure yet. Your team gives you the benefit of the doubt, for now. That's earned goodwill, not guaranteed loyalty. Identify which pillars are sitting at the higher end of this range and give them deliberate attention before they drift into fragile territory.

If 1–2 pillars scored 5–6: Targeted trust drift is emerging. These pillars are sending early signals that your team is already reading. Name the specific behaviors driving the score within 10 days and begin correcting them within 30 days before isolated drift becomes a systemic pattern.

If 3–4 pillars scored 5–6: Trust drift is no longer isolated; it's becoming systemic. Your team isn't guessing whether something is off. They know. Prioritize the pillar with the highest score, name the driving behaviors within 10 days, and begin visible repair within 30 days. Then sequence the remaining fragile pillars across the next 90 days. Drift at this scale doesn't self-correct. It accelerates.

If any pillar scored 7+: That pillar isn't fragile. It's broken. Your team has already made their assessment about your leadership in this area, and they're making decisions based on those conclusions, not waiting for you to catch up. Begin repair immediately using the frameworks in Part IV. The longer a broken pillar stays unaddressed, the more it contaminates the pillars still standing.

If 4+ pillars scored 7+: This isn't a trust problem. This is a leadership crisis. Your team has moved past frustration into self-protection; they're working around you, not with you. Incremental repair won't reach this. You need a full system reset. Turn to the 90-Day Trust Build™ in Chapter 16 and commit to the process without shortcuts. At this stage, the only thing more costly than rebuilding trust is continuing to lead without it.

What's Next

Now that you can diagnose where trust is leaking, the next seven chapters explain how to strengthen each pillar before fractures become failures. Each chapter provides the principle behind the pillar, the behaviors that build or break it, real leadership moments that test it, and Your System Check.

A note about who this audit serves most. If you already know trust is broken, you probably know where to start. The leaders this tool serves best are the ones in the middle, scoring in the 3–4 and 5–6 ranges. Not broken. Not failing. Drifting. And drift is the most dangerous place to lead from, because it feels like everything is fine from the inside while your team sees it differently.

Your System Check:

- *Based on your Trust Audit™, which pillar scored the highest (most warning signs)?*
- *That's the pillar breaking trust fastest right now.*
- *Name it. You'll address it in the next 72 hours.*
- *(The 72-hour standard is introduced in full in Chapter 9; hold it in mind as you audit.)*

Quick Reference: Signal Response Scripts + Tracking Dashboard

When you see a signal, use these scripts immediately. Track signals monthly using the dashboard below. Three or more negative trends indicate active trust fracture.

IMMEDIATE ACTION

"I've noticed people are asking permission for things I expect you to have ownership of. Let me clarify: Here's what you're empowered to decide without checking with me: [list]. Here's what requires my input: [list]. If you're unsure, ask. But my goal is for you to own decisions in your domain."

IMMEDIATE ACTION

"I've noticed questions have dropped off. That's a problem. If you're not asking, I'm either not creating safety, or I'm not being clear. Which is it? Then listen. Don't defend."

IMMEDIATE ACTION

"I've been checking work I used to trust. That's on me. Here's what's changing: I'm stepping back. If the system isn't working, we'll fix the system, not add more oversight."

IMMEDIATE ACTION

"I've noticed you're not volunteering like you used to. How's your capacity? Am I overloading you?" Then act on what you hear. Remove work. Redistribute load.

IMMEDIATE ACTION

"I know there are rumors about [topic]. Here's what I know: [facts]. Here's what I don't know yet: [gaps]. Here's when I'll have more: [timeline]."

IMMEDIATE ACTION

"I've noticed issues are surfacing late. That's a problem. I need bad news early, not late. If you're hesitating to bring me problems, what would make it safer?" Then change whatever that is.

IMMEDIATE ACTION

"I'm hearing that conversations are happening without me. That tells me either I'm not creating safety or I'm not responding well when people bring me hard truths. Which is it?"

IMMEDIATE ACTION

Conduct a full Trust Audit™ (Chapter 2). Identify the first fracture. Address it immediately using the 72-Hour Repair Protocol™ (Chapter 12).

The Trust Signal Dashboard™

Use this dashboard to track signals monthly. If three or more signals are trending negative, trust is fracturing.

Signal	Month 1	Month 2	Month 3	Trend
Permission-seeking increasing?				
Questions decreasing?				
Execution slowing?				
High performers withdrawing?				
Rumors increasing?				
Problems surfacing late?				
Conversations happening "around" you?				
Emotional reactions disproportionate?				

(Note: This dashboard reappears in Chapter 11 with the full signal-by-signal diagnostic application.)

PART TWO—THE SEVEN PILLARS

CHAPTER 3: CHARACTER—VALUES WHEN THEY ARE EXPENSIVE

Character is not what you believe. It's what you do when your values conflict with convenience.

Anyone can claim values. Posters on walls. Statements in meetings. Words in strategy documents. But values are only real when they cost something.

Character is values under pressure.

"Put enough pressure on a leader, and you won't hear their talking points. You'll see their values."—Gearl Loden

The Test of Character

Character is revealed in three situations:

Situation 1: When Doing the Right Thing Is Personally Costly

"It's easy to do the right thing when doing the right thing costs nothing."

Character is tested when the right thing requires admitting you were wrong publicly, apologizing face-to-face, absorbing a financial loss, disappointing stakeholders, or delaying a win to do something properly.

Test: When was the last time you chose values over convenience, and it cost you something? If you can't answer that, it's a bigger problem than you think.

Situation 2: When No One Is Watching

Public integrity is performance. Private integrity is character.

Leaders with character follow through on commitments even when no one will know if they don't, correct mistakes even when they could be hidden, and treat people well even when there's no audience.

Test: Do you behave the same way when no one is watching as you do when everyone is?

Situation 3: When Violating Values Would Solve a Problem

The sharpest test of character is when breaking a value would fix an immediate crisis. You could blame someone else and protect yourself. You could hide information to avoid conflict. You could bend a rule to hit a deadline.

Leaders with weak character make exceptions when pressed. Leaders with strong character hold values even when it's painful.

How Character Breaks

Character breaks in three predictable ways:

Erosion Pattern 1: Stating Values But Not Enforcing Them

Leaders put values on websites, in handbooks, and in strategy decks. But values aren't tested in planning meetings. They're tested in budget cuts, in staffing shortages, and in the moments when honoring the value costs something real. That's when "transparency" shifts to "they're not ready to hear this." That's when "every client matters" shifts to "let's focus where we'll see results."

The Fix: Only state values you're willing to enforce when it's expensive. If you're not willing to enforce it, don't claim it.

When you are out of alignment, your team already sees it.

Erosion Pattern 2: Applying Standards Selectively

Character breaks when leaders enforce values for some people but not others. High performers get exceptions. Long-tenured employees get grace. Employees with connections have special privileges. Leadership gets flexibility that others don't.

The Fix: Apply values consistently, or admit they're not really values. If "accountability" is a value, it applies to everyone, including you. If "respect" is a value, it applies in every interaction, not just with people who have power.

Erosion Pattern 3: Bending Values "Just This Once"

The most dangerous phrase in leadership: "Just this once." "Just this once, we'll skip the safety protocol to meet the deadline." "Just this once, we'll approve the expense without documentation." "Just this once, we'll let the behavior slide."

The first exception feels justified. The second feels necessary. The third becomes normal.

The Fix: If you're making an exception, ask, "Would I make this exception if it became public?" If not, don't make it.

The Commitment Test

Character is revealed through commitment over time. Anyone can act with integrity for a day, a week, or a month.

Character is acting with integrity when no one is watching, when the cost is high, when you're exhausted, and when it's been years, not weeks.

> In your chair, that kind of sustained commitment looks different, but it costs the same. It is the leader who keeps protecting what matters most when the pressure to pivot never stops. It is the executive who holds the hiring standard when urgency argues for an exception. Character is not what you do in the defining moment. It is what you do on the next ordinary Tuesday.

Character vs. Reputation

Character is who you are when no one is watching. Reputation is who people think you are.

Leaders often confuse the two. They manage reputation, what people see, without building character, who they actually are.

A reputation without character is fragile. One mistake, one leaked email, or one inconsistent decision, and reputation collapses.

Character, on the other hand, compounds. When you act with integrity consistently, even when no one is watching, people sense it. They may not be able to articulate why they trust you, but they do.

Character is rarely tested by dramatic, headline-grabbing dilemmas. It's tested in the quiet moments when no one would notice if you took the easier path. The two scenarios that follow put you in exactly those moments.

Trust in Action: Two Moments That Test Communication

Moment: The Mistake That Went Public

Context: You're a CEO. Your company made a pricing error that went live on the website. Hundreds of customers bought a product at 40% below cost. Legally, you could cancel the orders. Ethically, it feels wrong. Financially, it will cost you.

The Trust Test: Do you cancel the orders and cite the error in the terms of service? Honor the orders and absorb the cost? Or offer partial discounts as a compromise?

Pillars Tested: Character, Courage

What Strong Leaders Do: They honor the mistake and explain why.

"We made a pricing error yesterday that went live for 6 hours. Hundreds of customers ordered at the incorrect price. Legally, we could cancel those orders. We're not going to. We're honoring every order at the price customers saw. This will cost us significantly, but our reputation is worth more than short-term profit. We made the mistake, not our customers. We're fixing our process so this doesn't happen again."

Why This Works: It acknowledges the mistake publicly, which shows accountability. It chooses values over convenience, which demonstrates character. It explains the reasoning, which builds trust externally. Plus, it commits to fixing the system, which demonstrates competence.

The Trust Leak: Leaders who hide behind legal fine print to avoid costly mistakes destroy customer trust. Short-term savings create long-term reputation loss.

Moment: The Personal Crisis During Crunch Time

Context: You're a CEO. It's launch week, the most critical week of the quarter. Your VP of Product's father just had a stroke. He's in the ICU. She needs to fly out immediately. She's apologizing, offering to work remotely from the hospital. "I know the timing is terrible."

You have three choices: Tell her to go and mean it, no work, no guilt, and no checking in. Tell her to go, but keep reaching out "just to stay aligned." Or let her decide, knowing she'll choose work over family because she's afraid of letting you down.

Pillars Tested: Care, Character, Courage

Option A costs you something real: a launch week without a key leader. Options B and C cost you something bigger; they teach your entire team that your mantra of "we care about our people" has conditions.

Strong leaders remove the choice. They say go; they mean it, and they make the launch work without her. That's not soft leadership. That's trust infrastructure.

The Conversation

"Stop. Your dad is in the ICU. That's the only priority right now. You're flying out today. You're not working remotely. You're not checking your email. You're not on call. I'll handle the launch coverage. This isn't a favor that I'm doing for you. This is what we do when someone's family is in crisis. You would do the same for me. Go. I'll text you once a day just to check on you, not work. Just you. We've got this."

The Trust Leak

Leaders who say "go, we'll be fine," but then text at 9 pm about a work decision teach the entire organization two things: care is conditional, and your family matters less than our deadlines.

Saying you care and acting as you care are different things. The trust damage isn't from the expectation; it's from the gap between words and actions.

Your System Check:

- *When was the last time you chose a value over convenience, and it cost you something?*
- *If you can't remember, your values might be slogans, not systems.*
- *What is one decision in front of you right now where your values and convenience are in conflict?*

Those scenarios test your values in the moment, but the most revealing character tests aren't dramatic. They're the slow, quiet erosions that happen when leaders rationalize small compromises, the ones nobody notices until everyone has.

LEADERSHIP IN PRACTICE: CHARACTER

Story 3.1—When Values Got Expensive

There's a particular kind of quiet that settles over an organization when a leader faces a values test. People may not know the specifics, but they sense the pressure. They feel the weight of the decision before it's made. And they watch, not necessarily with suspicion, but with attention. Because in those moments, people aren't measuring strategy. They're measuring character.

One leader I coached faced that kind of moment.

A shortcut was available. The shape of the dilemma was universal. A faster path existed that would have improved results quickly. It would have looked good on paper. It would have satisfied short-term stakeholders, but it would have violated the values his organization had written on its walls: fairness, transparency, and stewardship.

He knew the shortcut would work. That's what made it tempting. In leadership, the distinction is where character lives, not in the easy moments where doing the right thing also happens to be the smart thing, but in the costly moments where integrity has a price tag and everyone in the room knows it.

He sat with it for two days. I know because we talked through both of those days. He wasn't wavering. He knew what he believed. He was calculating the cost of living by what he believed, and he was trying to make sure he could carry it.

That's the part of character that leadership books often skip. The decision isn't the hard part. The hard part is absorbing the consequences. He knew that choosing the principled path would cost time, possibly money, and almost certainly some political capital with people who wanted the faster result.

We didn't debate morality. That would have been the wrong conversation. The values were clear. What he needed wasn't moral clarity; he had that. What he needed was a system for making the decision visible so the organization didn't just see what was decided but understood why.

He communicated four things: the value at stake, in human language rather than corporate phrasing; why that value mattered now, not abstractly but concretely; the trade-off he was willing to make by choosing the slower, costlier path; and what that choice would preserve in the long run: credibility, fairness, and a culture where people want to belong.

Then he backed it with one visible decision that proved it wasn't talk, one concrete action the entire organization could point to and say, "He chose the harder road, and he did it publicly."

The response wasn't an immediate celebration. Character decisions rarely generate applause in the moment. What they generate is something quieter and more durable: respect. In the weeks that followed, that respect converted into trust.

Engagement increased because people could trust that leadership wasn't transactional. In organizations where leaders consistently choose expediency over values, people learn to hedge. They protect themselves because they can't predict what the leader will sacrifice next. When a leader absorbs cost to protect a value, that calculation changes. People stop hedging and start investing.

Performance stabilized because the organization stopped spending energy questioning motives. When people trust the leader's character, they don't waste cognitive bandwidth wondering whether the latest initiative has a hidden agenda. They can focus on the work.

Even people who disagreed with the specific decision respected the transparency. That's the most important lesson. Character doesn't require everyone to agree with your choice; it requires them to trust your process. When people can see the reasoning, the values, and the willingness to pay the price, they can disagree and still follow. That's the kind of trust that survives difficulty.

"I knew there were people above me who wanted me to make the quickest and easiest decision, and I knew the right decision wasn't it. Doing the right thing was expensive. But it bought something I couldn't have gotten any other way."

Character isn't what you believe when leadership is easy. It's what you choose when leadership gets expensive. People are always watching to see whether you'll pay the bill.

Story 3.2—The Report He Didn't Have to Fix

The number was close enough. That was the honest truth, and he knew it.

He had submitted the quarterly performance report to the board three days earlier. The data was solid. The narrative was clean. The board had received it without a single question, which, in his experience, was the highest form of approval a governance document could receive.

Then he found the error.

It wasn't fraud. It wasn't even technically wrong. One metric, for a high-visibility program, had been framed against a comparison year that made the result look stronger than the fuller picture supported. Not falsified. Selectively presented. The kind of thing that happens when someone on your team is trying to make the results look favorable, and you're moving fast, and it looks fine on the surface because it is fine, roughly speaking, it is.

No one had caught it. No one was going to catch it. The next board meeting was six weeks out. By then, the report would be filed, the quarter would be closed, and this metric would be a footnote in a binder that nobody opened again.

He called me that afternoon.

"I need to think through something," he said.

I've learned that when a leader opens a call that way, the thinking is mostly already done. What they need is someone to confirm that what they're about to do is worth the cost.

He walked me through the error. I asked him two questions. The first: Was the information misleading? He was quiet for a moment. "If a board member used it to make a decision about the program, yes. It would point them in the wrong direction."

The second question: Who would you be if you let it stand?

He didn't answer that one out loud. He didn't need to.

What made this hard wasn't the correction itself. Sending a follow-up to the board with a revised metric and a brief explanation is, on paper, a simple act. What made it hard was everything that surrounded it. He had spent two years rebuilding trust with a board that had been burned by a predecessor who managed data the way politicians manage optics: carefully, selectively, in service of a narrative rather than a reality. He had been hired specifically because he was different, because he was someone the board could trust to tell them the truth even when the truth was uncomfortable.

Coming forward meant reopening a conversation the board thought was closed. It meant admitting that something had slipped through his review. It meant risking the credibility he had built in a context where credibility was the entire foundation of his leadership.

Staying quiet meant none of that. It meant keeping the momentum, protecting the relationship, and carrying a small private compromise that, in the scheme of things, didn't change much.

He sent the correction.

Not a long email. Not a dramatic confession. A short, direct message: a revised figure, the context for the discrepancy, and a sentence acknowledging that his review process should have caught it before submission.

The board chair responded within an hour. Two sentences. Thank you for flagging this. This is exactly why we trust you.

That response matters, but it isn't the point of the story.

The point is what happened to him internally before he sent it. The calculation he ran and what he concluded from it. He told me afterward: "I kept trying to convince myself it wasn't that big of a deal. And then I realized that the fact that I was trying to convince myself meant it was."

That's the diagnostic many leaders miss. When you find yourself building a case for why something is acceptable, pay attention to the rationalization. That's where Character starts making exceptions for itself. Character doesn't fracture dramatically. It fractures in the moments when you're deciding whether to notice something or not.

The need to build a case is itself a red flag.

The correction cost him an uncomfortable 24 hours. It bought him something the board couldn't have given him any other way: the knowledge that his integrity wasn't conditional on whether anyone was watching.

Story 3.3—The Slow Compromise Leader

I've been in coaching rooms where character drift was subtle and private. But I want to share a pattern I've observed repeatedly across industries, because when it plays out at scale, the consequences are impossible to ignore.

These stories show up in the news as sudden falls. They're not. They're the final frame of a film that started rolling years earlier.

Inevitably, the pattern is the same. It doesn't start with corruption. It starts with convenience. It starts with a series of small compromises that feel reasonable in the moment until the distance between stated values and actual behavior becomes too large to sustain.

The erosion follows the same sequence. Pressure arrives, not a single crisis, but a sustained squeeze. Budget constraints that don't ease. Timelines that keep compressing. Stakeholders who want results without providing resources. The kind of pressure that doesn't break you in a day but wears you down over months.

The first compromise is small. A reporting shortcut that saves time but skips a verification step. The leader knows the numbers are "close enough." They tell themselves they'll go back and tighten the process when things calm down.

Things don't calm down.

The second compromise is slightly larger. A hiring decision that bypasses the standard vetting process because the timeline is tight and the candidate is "good enough." The leader tells themselves the urgency justifies the shortcut.

The third compromise is a commitment made to the team about workload protection that quietly gets abandoned when a new initiative lands. No announcement. No acknowledgment. Just a slow shift in expectations that everyone feels but no one names.

Each decision has a reasonable justification. That's what makes this failure mode so dangerous. The leader doesn't wake up one morning and decide to abandon their values. Their values erode gradually, one "just this once" at a time. Each compromise makes the next one easier. It's not that the leader stopped caring. Rather, the distance between where they are and where they started grows so gradually that they lose sight of how far they've drifted.

This is why character isn't sustained through willpower alone. It's sustained through structures that make drift visible before it creates damage.

Character holds when leaders build structures around it, specific behavioral standards with clear boundaries, instead of aspirational language.

"We don't skip the verification step, regardless of timeline." "We don't bypass vetting, regardless of urgency." Written down. Visible. Referenced in real decisions. When the standard is concrete, deviation becomes recognizable. When it's vague, anything can be justified.

Committing to standards isn't enough. Every leader needs a named accountability partner, someone with explicit permission to say "you're drifting" without fear of consequence. Not a yes-person. Not a critic. Someone who respects the leader enough to protect them from themselves. The sentence that saves careers isn't dramatic. It sounds like this: "I've noticed we're making exceptions to our own standards, and I'm worried about where that leads."

Then there's the practice most leaders resist, a quarterly values audit. Not a compliance exercise. A genuine reflection: where did I compromise this quarter? What pressure drove it? Would I make the same decision if it were public?

That last question is the sharpest diagnostic for character drift. If you don't want the decision on the front page, it's not aligned with your values no matter how reasonable it felt at the moment.

Character doesn't fail in dramatic moments. It fails in the ordinary ones, the small decisions that feel insignificant but compound into something never intended. The system you build around your values matters more than the strength of your convictions. Because convictions, under enough pressure and without enough structure, bend. Systems hold.

I have sat with leaders at every point on that arc. Some came early, after the first compromise, unsettled enough to name it. Some came later, after the pattern had been running long enough that the people around them had already noticed what the leader had not yet admitted. In every case where the drift was caught before it became a fall, there was a common thread. Not exceptional willpower. Not a stronger moral code than the leaders who did not catch it. What they had was someone willing to say it out loud before it was too late. A peer. A coach. A board member.

Someone with enough trust in the relationship and enough courage in the moment to say, "I need to tell you something. I think we are starting to drift, and I am not sure you can see it from where you are standing."

That sentence has saved more careers than any compliance program ever written. Build the structures. Name the standards. And then find the person who will say it to you when you cannot say it to yourself.

CHAPTER 4: CONSISTENCY—THE FOUNDATION OF PREDICTABILITY

"People don't follow the leader they admire. They follow the leader they can predict." —*Gearl Loden*

Consistency is the proof that character is real.

Without it, values are slogans, not systems.

You can communicate brilliantly, but if you contradict yourself, people stop listening. You can demonstrate competence, but if your behavior is erratic, people won't rely on your systems. You can care deeply, but if your care is inconsistent, people will doubt it's real.

When people can predict how you'll respond, they can relax, plan, and act without constantly checking with you. When they can't, every decision becomes a guess, and every interaction carries risk.

Consistency is not about being rigid. It's about being predictable in ways that matter.

What Consistency Actually Means

Consistency doesn't mean never changing your mind, treating every situation identically, or being inflexible. Consistency is responding to similar situations similarly, explaining when you change approaches, and holding standards even when it's inconvenient.

People don't need you to be perfect. They need to know what to expect.

The Three Forms of Consistency

Form 1: Behavioral Consistency

Do you respond the same way to the same stimulus?

If someone brings you a problem on Monday, do you respond with curiosity? But when they bring you a problem on Friday, do you respond with frustration?

If you say "bring me issues early" but then react defensively when someone does, your behavior is inconsistent, and people learn not to bring you issues.

Test: Would your team describe your responses as predictable or as "depends on the day"?

Form 2: Standards Consistency

Do the rules apply evenly?

If you enforce a deadline for one person but extend it for another without explanation, people conclude standards are negotiable.

If you hold one team member accountable for attendance but excuse another, people conclude that enforcement depends on favoritism.

Consistency doesn't mean zero flexibility. It means explaining when and why you make exceptions.

Test: If you make exceptions, can people predict when and why, or does it feel arbitrary?

Form 3: Values Consistency

Do your actions match your stated values under pressure?

If you say "people first" but expect someone to work through a family crisis, your values are inconsistent.

If you say "transparency matters" but withhold information when it's uncomfortable, your values are inconsistent.

Values consistency is tested when values become costly.

How Consistency Breaks

Consistency breaks in three predictable ways:

Erosion Pattern 1: Pressure-Induced Drift

When pressure increases, leaders often shift behavior without realizing it. They micromanage work they used to trust. They skip explanations to save time. They bend standards to meet deadlines. They react emotionally instead of calmly.

The leader thinks, "I'm adapting to the situation."

The team feels that, "Leadership is unpredictable now."

The Fix: When pressure increases, narrate what you're doing and why. This explanation doesn't eliminate the behavior change, but it makes it predictable.

Erosion Pattern 2: Exception Creep

Leaders make exceptions with good intentions: "Just this once, we'll skip the approval process." "Just this time, we'll let the deadline slide." "Just for them, we'll waive the requirement."

The first exception feels reasonable. The second feels necessary. The third becomes the new normal. *Eventually, there's no standard, just a series of exceptions.*

The Fix: Name exceptions when you make them. Explain why. Confirm they're temporary.

Erosion Pattern 3: Unannounced Standard Changes

Sometimes standards need to change. Markets shift. Priorities evolve. Constraints tighten.

The problem isn't changing standards. The problem is changing them without explanation.

When leaders change standards silently, people conclude that leadership doesn't know what they're doing, that standards were never real to begin with, or that the new standard will probably change too.

The Fix: Announce standard changes before enforcing them.

"We're changing the approval threshold from $10K to $5K effective next month. Here's why: we've seen a pattern of budget overruns on mid-range purchases that weren't getting enough scrutiny. Here's what that means for you: any purchase between $5K and $10K now goes through the same review as $10K-plus requests. Questions?"

The Mental Traffic Problem

Inconsistency creates mental traffic.

When people can't predict how you'll respond, they spend energy gaming scenarios, checking with peers about your last mood, and overexplaining to protect themselves.

In high-trust environments, people spend that energy solving problems. In low-trust environments, they spend it managing the leader.

Consistency in Practice: The Leaders Who Shaped Me

One of the most powerful forms of leadership development is not found in a classroom or a book. It is found in proximity to a leader who lives what they teach. Early in my career, I was supervised by a leader who modeled consistency with precision. Later I was able to supervise several others who did the same. Watching them shaped me in ways no curriculum could.

What I observed in each of them was not perfection. It was predictability. The same standards, the same tone, the same expectations on both a good day and on a hard one, when the organization was thriving and when it was under pressure. You always knew where they stood, and that knowing created something that is difficult to manufacture: trust.

Those leaders helped me become more consistent. Not by telling me what consistency looked like, but by showing me what happened when someone actually lived it.

During COVID, our team faced a communication challenge that most organizations were not prepared for. The pace of change was relentless, the uncertainty was real, and every communication decision carried weight. What our team built, across multiple touchpoints and through multiple difficult moments, was recognized and praised for its consistency. Not because we had all the answers. Because people knew how we would show up. They could count on us to communicate the same way on day one of a crisis as they could on day ninety.

Here is what I have come to believe about consistency, and what I share with every leader I coach: consistency does not mean agreement. Your team will not always agree with your decisions, and that is fine. What they need is to know what to expect from you, day in and day out, when times are good and when times are stressful. Consistency is not about being liked. It is about being known.

You do not have to agree with someone to trust them.
You just have to know what to expect.

Consistency in Practice: Fred Rogers

Fred Rogers hosted Mister Rogers' Neighborhood for 33 years.

Every episode opened the same way. Fred walked through the door, sang the same song, changed into a cardigan and sneakers, and greeted the audience with the same warmth. The format was so consistent that it became a cultural reference.

Why?

Because consistency creates safety.

Children watching knew what to expect. The predictability allowed them to relax and engage with the content.

Adults mocked the predictability, but children trusted it.

The same principle applies to leadership.

Predictability isn't boring. It's the foundation that makes everything else possible.

The principles above give you the framework. But trust isn't built in frameworks; it's built in moments. The two scenarios that follow will test how you apply consistency when the pressure is real and the stakes matter.

Trust in Action: Two Moments That Test Consistency

Moment: The Promotion That Surprised Your Team

Context: You're a CEO who just promoted someone internally. The person is capable, but the promotion bypassed two people your team expected to advance. You made the decision based on strategic fit that isn't obvious from the outside. Your team is confused and frustrated.

The Trust Test: Do you defend the decision by listing the promoted person's strengths? Do you acknowledge the surprise and explain the criteria used? Do you ask your team to "trust the process" without explanation?

Pillars Tested: Clarity, Communication, Consistency

What Strong Leaders Do: They explain the decision criteria without diminishing others.

"I know this wasn't the decision some of you expected. Let me explain what drove it. This role requires someone who can build cross-functional partnerships quickly while managing ambiguity. That's a specific capability, and it's not a judgment on anyone else's value. Here's how I evaluated fit: [specific criteria]. I should have communicated

these criteria before the decision was made; that's on me. Going forward, I'll make promotion criteria visible before decisions are finalized."

Why This Works: It acknowledges the surprise and validates their experience. It names the specific criteria, which reduces the perception of favoritism. It owns the communication gap and takes responsibility. And it commits to future transparency, which ensures it doesn't happen again.

The Trust Leak: Leaders who say "You'll understand eventually" or "Just trust me" without explanation create cynicism. People don't need to agree, but they need to understand.

Moment: The Standard That's Been Sliding

Context: You're a team leader. Meeting start times have become suggestions. People drift in 5–10 minutes late. You've let it slide because "everyone's busy." Now it's normalized.

The Trust Test: Do you keep letting it slide to avoid seeming rigid? Reestablish the standard clearly and immediately? Or call out individuals publicly to make an example?

Pillars Tested: Consistency, Courage, Clarity

What Strong Leaders Do: They reset the standard without shaming.

"I need to address something I've let slide: meeting start times. We used to start on time. We don't anymore. That's on me; I didn't address it when it started. Here's what's changing: meetings start at the stated time. If you're going to be late, send a message. If lateness becomes a pattern, we'll address it directly. This starts with our next meeting. I'm not upset about what's happened; I'm clarifying what happens next."

Why This Works: It owns the drift instead of blaming the team. It states the standard clearly and removes ambiguity. It applies going forward with no retroactive punishment. And it commits to enforcement, which makes it real.

The Trust Leak: Leaders who let standards erode quietly create confusion. People don't know what matters anymore.

Diagnosing Your Consistency

Answer these questions:

Behavioral Consistency:

- Would your team describe your responses as "predictable" and not as "it depends on the day"?
- When pressure increases, does your behavior remain steady enough that your team knows what to expect?

Standards Consistency:

- When you make exceptions, can people predict when and why?
- Do you enforce standards evenly? Would your team agree?

Values Consistency:

- When your stated values conflict with convenience, do your stated values win?
- Can people point to examples where your values held even when they were expensive?

If you can't answer "yes" confidently to these questions, consistency is your fracture point.

Your System Check:

- *Can your team predict how you will respond when similar situations arise?*
- *If not, what will you explain in the next 48 hours?*

These scenarios illustrate the tension. Now let's look at how consistency plays out over time, not in isolated moments but in the patterns that quietly build or erode trust across weeks and months. The following stories come from my leadership experiences and coaching practice and are drawn from real leaders navigating real trust fractures.

LEADERSHIP IN PRACTICE: CONSISTENCY

Story 4.1—The "Different Rules" Leader

The team looked productive from a distance.

That's the phrase I kept coming back to as I sat with this leader for the first time. On paper, the numbers were moving. Projects were closing. The weekly reports told a story of a functioning team doing respectable work.

But he hadn't called me because things were going well. He'd called because something felt wrong, and he couldn't name it.

"I don't think people trust me," he said. Then, immediately, "That's not right either. I think they trust me as a person. They just don't trust… the system."

I asked what that looked like day to day.

The answer came slowly. People had stopped volunteering ideas in meetings. Initiative had narrowed; team members did exactly what was asked and nothing more. Performance wasn't crashing. It was becoming cautious. Safe. Predictable in the worst way.

So I started listening. Not to the leader but to the team.

What I heard wasn't anger. It wasn't a rebellion. It was something quieter and more corrosive: resignation.

One team member put it plainly: "There are different rules for different people. Everyone knows it. Nobody says it."

That's the sentence that told me what I was dealing with.

The leader had standards. They were written down, discussed in onboarding, and referenced in reviews. But they weren't applied consistently. A few high performers could miss deadlines, skip processes, or bend norms and stay in good standing. Others were corrected quickly for smaller issues. Nobody used the word "favorites." But everybody behaved as though favorites existed. Because functionally, they did.

Here's what leaders often miss about inconsistency: it doesn't just create unfairness; it creates a tax. People start spending energy reading the room instead of doing the work. They calculate risk before they speak. They hedge instead of committing. And over time, the best people, the ones with the most options, start pulling back. Not dramatically, just enough to protect themselves. Some will even leave the company.

That's what was happening here. The team wasn't disengaged because they lacked motivation. They were disengaged because the rules weren't real.

I told him something he didn't expect: "Your team doesn't need more inspiration. They need to know the rules apply to everyone, including the people you like most."

That landed hard. It was supposed to.

We started with one move. Not a policy overhaul. Not a speech about values. One visible standard, stated publicly: "Here's what we can all count on going forward."

Then we built a consistency map, a simple document that made expectations observable: what "good" looks like, described in behaviors, not intentions, what happens when the standard is met, what happens when the standard is missed, and critically, what triggers an exception and who approves it.

That last piece changed everything. We created an exception protocol. Exceptions weren't banned. That would be rigid, not consistent. But if an exception was requested, the leader had to name what standard was being bent, why it was being bent, and how fairness would be protected. Exceptions could happen. They just couldn't happen in secret.

The leader shared his goal with his team and, within the first few weeks, made three deliberate decisions that proved the standard was real. Same response. Same follow-through. Regardless of who was involved. One of those decisions was particularly hard; it involved a high performer operating outside the standard without consequence for years. The leader held the standard anyway. Not with aggression. With clarity.

The shift didn't happen overnight. But by 90 days, you could see and feel significant shifts across the organization.

Engagement rose because people stopped bracing for surprise. Performance improved because teams stopped wasting energy reading his mood or guessing whether standards would apply today. He reported fewer escalations, fewer side conversations, faster execution, and a stronger employee retention rate, not because the team worked harder but because the environment became predictable.

And here's what made it stick: as he practiced consistency, he also sharpened his communication and clarity around expectations. Those three disciplines reinforced each other. Consistency gave communication credibility. Communication gave clarity a vehicle. Clarity gave consistency a visible standard to hold. Over time, he became strong across all three, and it showed. Not just in the day-to-day rhythm of the team, but in their cultural surveys. The numbers told the story the hallways had already been telling: people felt safer, more aligned, and more willing to invest discretionary effort because the system had become trustworthy.

One team member said it best during a check-in: "I finally feel like I can just do my work and know what to expect."

Every leader who has ever dismissed consistency as a soft issue should sit with that sentence.

When people can't "just do their work" because the system is unreliable, every hour of productivity carries a hidden surcharge of anxiety and calculation.

The team didn't need more motivation. They needed to know the rules were real.

Story 4.2—The "Mood-Tax"

The first thing the team told me, not in those words, but in a dozen small ways, was that their leader had become as unpredictable as the weather.

You'd hear it in how people described their mornings: "Let's see what kind of day it's going to be." You'd see it in how meetings started, often tentatively, watchfully, reading the room before committing to honesty. You'd feel it in the hallways, where side conversations weren't gossip but a survival strategy: "Did you hear what happened? What do you think it means?"

The leader was highly capable. Deeply committed. Visibly present. No one questioned her intelligence or her care for the organization.

What they questioned was predictability.

Priorities shifted based on the last conversation she had. Agreements made in one meeting were quietly revised in another. Projects launched with conviction on Monday and lost momentum by Thursday. The team had learned, through painful repetition, that committing early was risky. If you invested too much too soon, you'd likely have to pivot, and the pivot wouldn't come with an explanation. It would just happen.

So the team adapted. They waited. They hedged. They stopped acting until they were certain the direction would hold. Initiative dropped. She interpreted this as hesitation, or laziness.

"I don't understand why everything takes so long," she told me. "I've given them clear direction."

"How many times?" I asked.

"What do you mean?"

"How many different clear directions have you given in the last 60 days?"

The silence was the answer.

This is one of the common trust patterns I encounter in coaching. The leader isn't erratic in her own mind. From her perspective, she's responding intelligently to changing conditions. She sees new information; she adjusts. That feels like agility. But from the team's perspective, it feels like chaos, because they can't tell which version of the plan is real, how long it will last, or whether their effort today will still matter tomorrow.

The gap between her intent and the team's experience was enormous, and it was growing every week.

We didn't start by telling her to be more consistent. That's too vague to be useful, and it usually just makes leaders self-conscious without giving them anything to do differently.

Instead, we built consistency into the workflow through establishing decision rules:

- Naming three criteria for what makes something a top priority, so she had to evaluate against a filter, not a feeling.
- A standing "pause point" before any priority could change, with a 24-hour minimum notice between a new idea and a new directive.
- And a weekly decision review where the team heard three things: what we decided, what changed since last week, and why.

That last piece was the discipline that changed everything. She stopped making decisions in private that affected people publicly. If a direction shifted, she had to name it out loud, explain the trade-off, and own the disruption it caused. No more disappearing agreements. The team was able to ask clarifying questions.

The first few weeks were uncomfortable. She felt constrained. "This slows me down," she said.

"It doesn't slow you down," I told her. "It keeps your speed from costing more than it produces."

Within 60 days of disciplined repetition, the team could feel a noticeable difference. Engagement increased because people could anticipate how decisions would be made. Performance improved because teams stopped waiting to see if the plan would survive the week. And something unexpected happened: her own stress decreased because when the system carried the weight of consistency, she didn't have to carry it alone through force of personality.

She learned something that takes most leaders years to internalize: consistency isn't repetition. It's readability.

When people can read their leader, they stop bracing and start building. That's the difference between compliance and commitment.

Consistency is the proof that Character is real and the foundation on which every other pillar stands. In the next chapter, we examine the pillar most critical to your team's ability to function under uncertainty: Communication.

CHAPTER 5: COMMUNICATION—REDUCING UNCERTAINTY

"The leader who controls information controls the room. The leader who shares it builds the team." —*Gearl Loden*

Communication is not about how much you say.

It's about how much uncertainty you remove.

When leaders communicate well, people know why decisions were made, what's changing and what isn't, what success looks like, and what happens next. When leaders communicate poorly, people fill the gaps with rumors, worst-case scenarios, and quiet plans to leave.

The quality of communication determines whether information reduces anxiety or multiplies it.

The Uncertainty Problem

Humans hate uncertainty more than bad news.

Tell someone "the project is canceled," and they'll be disappointed, then move on. Tell someone "We're reviewing the project and will decide soon," and they'll spend weeks anxious, distracted, and speculating.

Uncertainty is cognitively expensive. When people don't know what's happening, they spend mental energy gaming scenarios, scanning messages for hidden meaning, and spreading rumors to reduce their own anxiety.

Good communication reduces that energy drain and builds trust faster.

What Good Communication Does

Good communication has three jobs:

Job 1: Explain the "Why" Before the "What" Surprises People

Most leaders announce decisions and then explain them when asked.

Strong leaders explain reasoning before decisions is announced.

Strong communication: *"We're restructuring the team because client needs have shifted from project-based to ongoing partnerships. That requires a different skill mix. Here's what's changing. Here's what's staying the same. Here's the timeline. Questions?"*

The strong version removes uncertainty. People may not like the decision, but they understand it.

Job 2: Communicate Proactively, Not Reactively

Weak leaders communicate when asked. Strong leaders communicate *before* being asked.

If people are asking, "What's happening with X?" you've already lost trust. They should have known before they had to ask.

Test: Are people asking for updates, or do you provide them before questions arise?

Job 3: Name Uncomfortable Truths Instead of Softening Them

Leaders often soften bad news to "protect" people, but softening creates confusion.

Strong communication: *"Budget cuts are coming. We don't know the final number yet, but we're planning for a 10–15% reduction. Here's the timeline for decisions. Here's what I'll share as I know more. Here's what you can control right now."*

Strong communication doesn't eliminate anxiety. It eliminates uncertainty, and uncertainty is worse.

How Communication Breaks

Communication breaks in three predictable ways:

Erosion Pattern 1: Withholding to "Protect" People

Leaders often withhold information with good intentions: "I don't want to worry them until I have all the facts." "I don't want to share bad news right before the weekend." "I'll wait until I have a solution, not just a problem."

But withholding doesn't protect people. It increases anxiety.

People sense when something is wrong. When leaders don't name it, people fill the gap with worst-case scenarios.

The Fix: Communicate what you know, when you know it, even if incomplete.

Partial information reduces uncertainty better than silence.

Erosion Pattern 2: Over-Explaining to Avoid Pushback

Some leaders over-communicate to preempt every possible objection. The message becomes so long and detailed that the core point gets lost.

Weak communication: *"As you know, we've been monitoring market conditions closely, and several factors have emerged that require us to reconsider our approach. First, customer preferences have shifted significantly in Q3, with a noticeable trend toward… [300 more words]… and therefore, we're pausing the initiative."*

Length doesn't equal clarity.

Strong communication: *"We're pausing the initiative. Customer needs shifted in Q3 and the model no longer fits. Here's what that means for your work: [two sentences]. Questions?"*

Erosion Pattern 3: Assuming People Know What You Know

Leaders live with information longer than their teams.

By the time leaders announce a decision, they've thought about it for weeks, discussed it in multiple meetings, and processed the reasoning internally so the decision feels self-evident to them. But for the team, it's brand new.

The Fix: Explain reasoning as if people haven't been in the room with you, because they haven't.

The Drip Decision Protocol™

Some decisions require time to finalize, but silence during the waiting period destroys trust.

The Drip Decision Protocol™ prevents trust erosion during decision-making.

Day 1: Announce that a decision is being made. "We're evaluating whether to continue the X initiative. The decision will be finalized within 30 days."

Day 10: Provide a progress update, even if nothing has changed. "Update: We're still evaluating. No decision yet. The timeline hasn't changed."

Day 20: Another update. "Update: We've narrowed it to two options. Final decision by the end of the month as planned."

Day 30: Announce the decision. "Decision made: We're discontinuing X. Here's why…"

Why this works:

> *"The decision rarely creates anxiety. The silence does."*

Regular updates, even if just "no update yet," eliminate the anxiety.

Speed vs. Precision

Leaders often delay communication to "get it right." An imperfect message delivered now builds more trust than a perfect message delivered later.

The only reason to wait: if the information will change significantly within 24–48 hours. Otherwise, communicate what you know now.

The principles above give you the framework. But communication isn't tested in calm conditions; it's tested in the moments when information is incomplete, emotions are high, and silence feels safer than speaking. The two scenarios that follow put you inside those moments, not to observe, but to decide.

Trust in Action: Two Moments That Test Communication

Moment: The Budget Cut You Can't Explain Yet

The context is education. The test is universal.

Context: You're a superintendent who just left a closed board meeting. The board voted to eliminate thirty-four positions across your district, including two central office positions, two assistant principals, two counselors, two social workers, fourteen teaching positions, and two programs loved by the community, effective at the end of the school year. Details are confidential until the agreed-upon date to begin notifying the people directly impacted and the official announcement in three weeks. Your building leaders are already asking questions. Rumors are spreading.

The Trust Test: Do you stay silent to honor confidentiality, knowing speculation will fill the gap? Do you share what you can without breaking board confidence? Do you acknowledge the tension without confirming details?

Pillars Tested: Character, Clarity, Communication

What Strong Leaders Do: They acknowledge the gap without violating trust.

"I know you're hearing things. I can't share details yet because the board process isn't complete. What I can tell you is this: we'll have clarity within two weeks, and when I can share more, you'll be the first to know. I'm not withholding to create suspense. I'm honoring a process. But I also hear your concern, and I'm not pretending it doesn't exist."

Why This Works: It names the reality that people are concerned about. It explains the constraint; the board process isn't complete. It commits to a specific timeline of two weeks. And it refuses to pretend everything is fine, which preserves credibility.

The Trust Leak: Leaders who say "Everything's fine, nothing to worry about" when people can see the boardroom tension create a trust vacuum. Silence doesn't protect trust, it erodes it.

Moment: The Decision That Arrived Without You

You're a chief nursing officer. The CEO and COO developed a strategic realignment plan, presented it to the board for strategic alignment, and moved forward with implementation. The plan eliminates the hospital's behavioral health service line and adds two new service lines, a Medical Weight Management/Metabolic Health Center and a Sports Medicine and Performance Center. The decision was made. The announcement went out. You were not in the room.

You found out the same way your nursing directors did.

Your phone starts ringing within the hour. Your directors want to know about the timeline and what this means for staffing. Your charge nurses are asking about redeployment. Your behavioral health nurses are scared about their jobs. And you have no answers because no one built the operational reality into the decision before they made it.

This is the moment that tests whether you lead with character or perform with it.

Option A: Enforce it without comment.

You forward the announcement. You tell your team to stand by for details. You keep your frustration contained and wait for direction from above.

This is not professionalism. It's self-protection dressed up as patience.

Your team doesn't just feel the decision. They feel your absence inside it. When a leader goes silent in a moment that demands presence, people don't assume neutrality. They assume you either knew and said nothing, or you didn't know and they don't matter. Either conclusion costs you.

Your behavioral health nurses are watching to see if their CNO will show up for them. Your directors are watching to see if you have any standing in this organization. Silence answers both questions in the wrong direction.

Option B: Signal your frustration to your team.

You let them know you weren't consulted. You make clear that cutting behavioral health without an operational plan is a mistake. You frame yourself as the one who would have done this differently.

This feels like advocacy. It isn't.

What you've done is transfer your institutional frustration onto the people who needed you to absorb it. Your behavioral health nurses are now managing their fear and your grievance. Your directors are now wondering whether the organization is structurally broken. And you've signaled to the CEO and board that you can't be trusted to execute decisions you didn't design.

But here's what leaders miss at this moment: you haven't just damaged trust with your team. You've damaged it with the leadership above you.

When you distance yourself from a decision you're responsible for executing, you signal that your loyalty is conditional. That you'll protect your own credibility before you'll protect the integrity of the institution. That you're a leader who vents when the decision is hard and shows up when it's easy.

Leadership is not a menu. You don't get to carry the authority and reject the accountability.

The CEO and COO are watching how you handle this, not because they're looking for compliance, but because they're looking for someone who can hold the line when it's uncomfortable. A CNO who signals downward that the problem came from above loses standing in both directions simultaneously.

Solidarity that requires you to betray the institution isn't solidarity. It's performance. And your team, over time, will recognize the difference.

Option C: Acknowledge the reality. Lead through it anyway.

This is the harder path. And it's the only one that holds.

It sounds like this:

"I know this landed without enough warning, and I hear your concern. I will be meeting with the CEO to learn the full rationale, understand the staffing plan, and make sure I am aligned in how I communicate this to you and how we implement it together. What I can tell you right now is this: the decision is real, the timeline is real, and my job is to make sure we navigate this in a way that protects our people and our

patients. Here's what I know. Here's what I don't know yet. Here's what I'm working to find out. And here's when you'll hear from me again."

That response does four things simultaneously. It validates the concern without amplifying the fear. It commits to going through the right channel to get answers. It signals that your priority is your people and your patients, not your position. And it gives your team something to hold onto while the uncertainty settles.

What this moment actually tests:

Not your loyalty to the C-suite. Not your popularity with your nursing directors.

It tests whether your communication is a leadership discipline or a defense mechanism.

Your team doesn't need you to have been in the room when the decision was made. They need to know you'll fight to get the information they need, tell them the truth about what you find, and stay present through the disruption.

That's the difference between a CNO people tolerate and one they trust.

Your System Check:

- *When a decision arrives that excludes you and lands hard on your team, do you lead through it or perform your way around it?*

Pillars Tested: Character, Communication, Courage

Diagnosing Your Communication

Answer these questions honestly

Proactive:

- Do you ensure your team knows what is coming before it arrives, or do they find out when everyone else does?
- Do you give your team information early enough that it changes how they prepare?
- Would your team agree that you keep them ahead of the curve, or would they say they are usually catching up?

Reactive:

- When your team does not understand your direction, do you look first at how you communicated before looking at how they listened?
- When a decision lands harder than you expected, do you go back and examine what you failed to communicate in advance?
- When people ask questions you expected them to already know the answers to, do you treat that as a communication failure rather than a listening failure?

Clarity:

- When people leave your meetings, do they act on what you intended vs. on what they assumed you meant?
- After you explain something, can people repeat back the core message in their own words without prompting?
- Do people ask clarifying questions freely, without hesitation?

Completeness:

- When the full picture would be uncomfortable to share, do you share it anyway?

- Do people on your team hear important information from you first, before they hear it from anyone else?
- When you share information, do people get the full picture or the version you were comfortable giving?

What your answers mean:

If your answers lean toward yes, your communication is functioning as a trust-building system. Your team is informed, prepared, and aligned. They are not filling gaps with speculation because you are not leaving gaps.

If your answers lean toward no, communication is your fracture point. Your team is operating on incomplete information, interpreting the direction differently than you intended, and building narratives to explain what you have not said. The trust cost is not dramatic. It is quiet and cumulative, and it compounds faster than most leaders realize.

If your answers are mixed, identify the category where the "no" answers cluster. A leader who is proactive but unclear is creating a different trust problem than a leader who is clear but reactive. The category tells you where to focus first.

Your System Check:

- *What will you explain in the next 24–48 hours, even if you do not have complete information?*

Those scenarios illustrate the immediate test, but communication failures seldom happen in a single moment. They accumulate over time, compounding into narratives that leaders never intended. The following stories show how that accumulation plays out and what it takes to reverse it.

LEADERSHIP IN PRACTICE: COMMUNICATION

Story 5.1—The Vacuum That Created a Story

The silence started with good intentions.

A leader I supported was navigating a difficult transition with high stakes, high visibility, and limited time. The kind of decision that touches every part of an organization and generates more questions than any one person can answer. She knew the stakes. She wanted to communicate responsibly. She wanted to have answers before she spoke.

So she waited.

The wait was supposed to be brief. A few days to finalize details, confirm the plan, and align the messaging. She told herself she was being responsible, that speaking too early would create confusion, and confusion would create fear.

What she didn't account for was that silence creates fear faster than confusion ever could.

By day three, the hallway conversations had started. Not malicious ones, anxious ones. "Have you heard anything?" "What do you think is happening?" "I heard that…" followed by something no one had actually said but someone had inferred from the silence.

By day five, the rumors had structure. They had details. They had emotional weight. The vacuum was being filled, not with facts, but with the most protective story people could construct: the version of events that explained why leadership wasn't talking and what that silence must mean.

Here's what I've learned about communication vacuums: they don't stay empty. They get filled by whoever has the most anxiety, the most access to fragments of information, and the most social influence to spread a narrative. And that person almost never has the clearest picture of reality.

By the time she was ready to communicate, she wasn't delivering news. She was competing with an established story. And that story had a head start.

The impact was measurable. Engagement dipped because uncertainty makes people self-protect. Performance slowed because teams didn't want to commit to work that might be reversed. Questions multiplied, not because people didn't trust her, but because they had lost trust in the information flow itself. When the pipeline goes dark, people stop trusting what comes out of it, even after it turns back on.

We didn't fix this with a speech. We fixed it with a cadence.

I introduced story ownership, a structured communication rhythm that she would hold regardless of whether she had full information. The cadence was simple and repeatable: what we know; what we don't know yet; what we're deciding; what we need from you; what happens next; and when you'll hear from me again.

That last step is significant and is often skipped. Because when people know when they'll hear from you, they stop filling in the gaps. The anxiety doesn't completely disappear, but at least it gets a container.

We also wrote three sentences she would repeat consistently, the same words, in the same order, in every setting. Not because people can't handle nuance, but because in times of uncertainty, a consistent message travels further and more accurately than an improvised one.

The organization needed to hear one story, not fragments pieced together from different versions of the same conversation.

The first communication went out within 72 hours. Not perfect. Not comprehensive. But structured, honest, and anchored by a promise of when the next update would come.

The cadence was held weekly for a month.

The shift was tangible. Engagement stabilized. Questions moved from private channels to open feedback loops, which meant she could address them directly instead of chasing shadows. Performance recovered because teams could plan with confidence, even if the plan was still evolving. And she stopped spending emotional energy fighting rumors and started spending that energy leading.

That experience reinforced something worth naming: silence is never neutral. In leadership, silence is a story someone else gets to write, and they will write the version that protects them, not the version that serves the organization.

Silence is never neutral.
In leadership, silence is a story someone else gets to write.

Her job wasn't to have all the answers before she spoke. It was to own the narrative early enough that the employees didn't have to invent one.

Story 5.2—The Noise Without Signal Leader

This one didn't look like a communication problem at first.

The leader was visible. Present. Available. He held regular meetings, sent frequent updates, and walked the floor. If you had measured communication by volume, he would have scored near the top of any organization I have worked with, and yet the team was confused.

Not uninformed. Confused. There's an important difference. Uninformed means people don't have enough data. Confused means they have too much data and not enough specificity. Every meeting brought new information, new context, and new observations, but without a clear hierarchy. People couldn't tell what mattered most, what was background, what required action, and what was just the leader thinking out loud.

"I thought communication and openness were my strengths," he told me. There was genuine bewilderment in his voice.

Everything looked fine from the outside; he was talking. People were listening. Meetings were happening, but underneath, teams were drowning in input and starving for direction.

Here's what was actually happening: the team had started treating every message from him with equal weight, because he hadn't taught them which messages carried more weight. A passing comment in a hallway carried the same authority as a formal directive in a meeting because his communication had no structure that differentiated the two.

The result was predictable. Rework increased; teams would pursue something he mentioned casually, only to discover it wasn't actually a priority. Engagement dropped because people stopped believing they could "get it right." No matter how hard they worked, they'd eventually discover they'd been solving the wrong problem, and the correction would come without him even realizing he'd caused the misfire.

We rebuilt communication around structure, not volume. The shift wasn't about talking less. It was about making every communication carry a clear signal.

He adopted a simple discipline for any important message: headline first, one sentence that says what this is about; three priorities only, because the human mind can hold about three active commitments before clarity degrades; and trade-offs named, not just what we're doing but what we're choosing not to do. He also clarified decision rights: who decides, who advises, and who executes; and a next touchpoint was scheduled so people know when the story continues.

We also introduced what I call a "repetition rule." If something is important, he says it the same way more than once. The same framing. The same words. Leaders often think repetition is weakness; it feels redundant, even insulting. But in organizations, repetition is how priority becomes real. When the message changes every time, even subtly, people recalibrate. When it stays the same, people commit.

Within 30 days, the change was visible, and by 90 days, the impact was undeniable.

Engagement improved because people finally knew what to focus on. Performance improved because teams stopped solving the wrong problems. Rework dropped. And something he didn't expect: his own message started traveling without distortion. When you give people a clear, repeatable frame, they carry it forward accurately. When you give them a stream of unstructured thoughts, they carry forward whatever fragment they remember most, which is almost never the fragment you intended.

Communication isn't measured by how much you say. It's measured by how well the system understands. If the system doesn't understand, the problem isn't their listening, it's your signal.

Communication is leadership made audible. When people understand, they act. When they're confused, they hedge. When they're left in a vacuum, they invent. Every pillar in this framework depends on information reaching people clearly, on time, and before speculation fills the gap. Communication is not one pillar among equals. It is the delivery system the other pillars run on. If the flow breaks down, everything built on top of it breaks with it.

Communication is not the softest pillar. It is the most load-bearing one. Character without communication is invisible. Courage without communication is just a private act. Clarity without communication is an idea that never lands. Leaders who master communication don't just reduce uncertainty. They create the conditions where every other discipline can do its work. But clear communication can only travel as far as the organization's competence allows. That is where Chapter 6 begins.

CHAPTER 6: COMPETENCE—SYSTEMS OVER HEROICS

"Competence isn't what you know. It's what your systems can do without you."
—Gearl Loden

Competence is not about being the smartest person in the room. It's about building systems that work without you.

When leaders confuse competence with personal capability, they create dependency. Decisions that shouldn't reach the leader do. The organization can't function when the leader is unavailable.

Personal competence matters. No system compensates for a leader who doesn't know the work. But personal competence alone isn't what separates good leaders from great ones. Systems do. Systems that produce reliable outcomes whether or not the leader is in the room.

The Two Forms of Competence

Form 1: Personal Competence Can you do the work? Do you have the knowledge, skills, and judgment the role demands?

This matters, especially early in leadership. But it becomes a liability if you can't move beyond it. Leaders who rely solely on personal competence become bottlenecks. They struggle to delegate. They burn out trying to do everything. They hire people less capable than themselves because capability feels like competition.

Test: *If you were unavailable for two weeks, would your team's execution collapse?* If yes, you haven't built competence; you've built dependency.

Form 2: Systemic Competence Can your organization produce results reliably, regardless of who's executing? Are you developing your people so your system gets stronger over time, not just maintained?

This is what trust requires. When outcomes depend on a leader's personal intervention, people conclude the system is fragile, execution is unpredictable, and success depends on luck or heroics. But when leaders build systems that work and invest in developing the team to run those systems, competence becomes institutional, not personal.

Test: *Do results vary significantly based on who's managing execution?* If yes, before calling it a people problem, look at the systems you have or haven't built around them.

If your organization only works when you're watching, you haven't built competence. You've built dependency.

How Competence Breaks

Competence breaks in three predictable ways:

Erosion Pattern 1: Promoting People Faster Than Capability Develops

Leaders promote high performers, but promotion without preparation creates competence gaps. The person struggles in the new role. Their team suffers. The leader has to step in constantly to compensate.

The Fix: Promote when someone has demonstrated capability in 70% of the new role's responsibilities.

If you promote someone before they're ready, provide scaffolding: clear success metrics, weekly coaching, defined decision authority, and a 90-day checkpoint.

But the deeper competence question isn't how you support someone after promotion. It's whether you're building the conditions for readiness before the promotion.

That's where internal job enrichment and leadership development programs become infrastructure. Leaders who identify and develop their next generation intentionally don't scramble when a role opens. They already know who's ready, who's close, and who needs another twelve months. They've been building that clarity through stretch assignments, cross-functional exposure, deliberate feedback loops, and investment in people before the organization needs them to perform.

The organizations that struggle most with competence gaps aren't failing at hiring. They're failing at cultivation. They promote from within reactively, then wonder why execution suffers. The pipeline was never built. The bench was never developed. And when a key leader leaves, the gap is felt immediately because no one was being prepared to fill it.

Internal development programs signal something beyond skill-building. They signal that the organization sees its people as worth investing in. That message builds trust long before a promotion ever happens.

Erosion Pattern 2: Building Processes Around Your Strengths (Not Transferable Systems)

Leaders will sometimes design processes that work for them, but only for them. A CEO who is great at relationship-building designs a sales process that depends on personal connections. When they hand it off, it fails.

The Fix: Design processes that average performers can execute successfully.

If only your top performers can make the system work, the system is broken.

Erosion Pattern 3: Rewarding Heroics Instead of Systems

Leaders often celebrate people who "save the day," but heroics are a symptom of system failure.

If someone has to work all weekend to meet a deadline, the system didn't plan for it. If someone has to personally intervene to fix a client issue, the system didn't catch it early enough.

The Fix: When heroics happen, ask, "What system would have prevented this from requiring heroics?" Then build that system.

Competence in Practice: Katherine Johnson

In 1962, NASA prepared to launch John Glenn into orbit.

The flight trajectory calculations were done by IBM computers, a new technology at the time. John Glenn refused to launch until Katherine Johnson, a NASA mathematician, verified the computer's calculations by hand.

Glenn reportedly said, "If she says they're good, I'm ready to go."

Why? Because Glenn trusted Johnson's competence more than he trusted the system.

Here's the critical lesson: Johnson didn't just verify the math. She helped NASA build systems that others could trust. By the time she retired, NASA's computational systems worked reliably without requiring her personal verification.

That's systemic competence.

The Capability–Commitment Diagnostic™

Performance problems usually come from one of two places: a capability issue or a commitment issue. Leaders who misdiagnose which one they are facing waste resources and erode trust.

CAPABILITY COMMITMENT	LOW CAPABILITY	HIGH CAPABILITY
HIGH COMMITMENT	**COACH & DEVELOP** *Low Capability + High Commitment* They want to succeed. Invest in training, mentorship, and structured growth. Build the capability the commitment has already earned.	**DELEGATE** *High Capability + High Commitment* Trust the system. Give autonomy, remove barriers, get out of the way. This is your highest-leverage talent.
LOW COMMITMENT	**REASSIGN OR REMOVE** *Low Capability + Low Commitment* Coaching won't fix this. The honest leadership decision is to move them out or into a fundamentally different role.	**DIAGNOSE ENGAGEMENT** *High Capability + Low Commitment* The issue isn't capability; it's engagement. Unsustainable workload? Wrong role? Trust already broken?

The Capability–Commitment Diagnostic™ · Loden Trust Framework™

The Common Misdiagnosis: Most leaders try to develop their way out of a commitment problem. That's a misdiagnosis. When the issue is engagement, not capability, more training doesn't build competence; it builds resentment.

The Trust Connection: Each quadrant requires a different leadership response. Applying the wrong intervention doesn't just waste time; it signals to the team that leadership can't diagnose what's actually happening.

The Competence Test

Ask yourself:

Execution Consistency:

• Do outcomes vary significantly based on who's executing?

• Can you predict results based on the person and not on the system?

Decision Escalation:

• Are decisions being escalated to you that shouldn't be?

• Do people ask permission for things they should own?

Capability Development:

• Are you promoting people before they're ready?

• Are you relying on people to "figure it out" instead of building a system that develops capability?

If you're answering 'yes,' competence is your fracture point.

Understanding competence as a concept is simple to understand. Living it as a discipline, especially when your personal capability outpaces the systems you've built, is where leaders often struggle. The two scenarios that follow test exactly that tension.

Trust in Action: Two Moments That Test Competence

Moment: The Decision You Made That You Now Realize Was Wrong

Context: You're a VP of Operations. Last month, you restructured the workflow process based on efficiency data. It's now clear that the new process is slower, more confusing, and frustrating for your team. You were confident it would work. It didn't.

The Trust Test: Do you defend the decision and wait for people to adapt? Reverse it immediately and acknowledge the mistake? Or adjust it quietly without acknowledging you were wrong?

Pillars Tested: Character, Courage, Competence

What Strong Leaders Do: They reverse and own it publicly.

"I need to address the workflow change we made last month. I was confident it would improve efficiency. I was wrong. The data I used didn't account for the implementation complexity, and the result has been slower work and more confusion. We're reverting to the previous process effective immediately. I should have piloted this with a small team before rolling it out broadly; that's a mistake I won't repeat. Thank you for your patience while I learned what you already knew."

Why This Works: It names the mistake specifically without hedging. It explains what was missed, which shows learning. It acts immediately, which demonstrates urgency. And it thanks the team, which acknowledges their experience.

The Trust Leak: Leaders who defend bad decisions long after they're proven wrong lose credibility fast. Recovery speed matters more than being right.

Moment: The Hiring Decision That Didn't Work Out

Context: You're a business leader. Four months ago, you hired someone into a senior role over internal objections. "Give them time," you said. It's now clear they're not a fit. Even with coaching and support, skill gaps are obvious, and the team is covering for them. You were wrong.

The Trust Test: Do you keep coaching them, hoping they'll improve? Act now to exit them respectfully? Or wait for them to fail visibly so the decision is easier?

Pillars Tested: Competence, Courage, Care

What Strong Leaders Do: They act quickly and own the hiring mistake.

"I need to talk about this role. I was confident this was the right hire. I was wrong. The skill gap is real, and asking the team to keep covering isn't fair to anyone, including the person in the role. I'm addressing this now. They'll transition out over the next 30 days, and we'll backfill with someone who has the capability this role requires. I own this, and I'll be more rigorous in future assessments."

Why This Works: It acts quickly instead of dragging it out. It owns the mistake publicly, which builds credibility. It protects the team, which demonstrates care. And it commits to a better process, which shows learning.

The Trust Leak: Every week that leaders delay removing someone who isn't performing, high performers lose faith. Competence gaps destroy trust when leaders won't address them.

Your System Check:

- *Was it a people problem where someone didn't have the capability or commitment? Or a system problem, where the process was broken?*
- *If it was a people problem, what development, coaching, or support is missing?*
- *If it was a system problem, what would you fix in the next 30 days?*
- *If it was both, which do you address first?*

Those scenarios test your judgment at the moment. But competence failures are usually systemic. They build over time as leaders rely on personal capability instead of organizational systems. The following stories show what that pattern looks like from the inside and how leaders I've coached have broken it.

LEADERSHIP IN PRACTICE: COMPETENCE

Story 6.1—The Smart Leader Who Couldn't Deliver

Everyone respected this leader. That was the first thing I heard when I started talking to the people around her. Brilliant. Strategic. Insightful. The kind of person who could walk into a room, read the dynamics in minutes, and offer a perspective that changed how people thought about the problem.

And yet, trust was slipping.

Not trust in her intelligence. Not trust in her intentions. Trust in her follow-through.

The pattern had been building for longer than anyone wanted to admit. Plans were strong. Kickoffs were energizing. She could paint a compelling picture of where the organization was headed, and people would leave the room believing. But then the weeks would pass, and the execution would drift. Deadlines moved, not with fanfare, but with quiet adjustments that people learned not to question. Initiatives started with energy and stalled without explanation. The next big idea would arrive before the last one had been completed.

The team had adapted in the most damaging way possible: they'd learned to hedge.

"Let's wait and see had become the team's operating system." People didn't invest fully in new directions because experience had taught them the direction wouldn't hold. They did enough work to appear compliant but held back the discretionary effort that turns good execution into great execution. Why pour yourself into something that might be abandoned next quarter?

Engagement dropped, not because people were unhappy, but because they'd lost faith that their effort would land somewhere real. Performance dropped because the organization kept restarting work. Resources were being consumed on launches, not on outcomes.

When she described the situation to me, she framed it as a motivation problem. "I don't think the team is bought in," she said. "I keep casting vision, and nothing sticks."

I told her something that reframed the entire engagement:

"Vision sticks when people trust that execution will follow. Right now, you've taught your team that the vision is temporary. So they treat their effort as temporary, too." —Gearl Loden

We didn't coach inspiration. We built an execution system.

Three measurable outcomes for the quarter, not seven, not ten. Three. And they had to be specific enough that anyone in the organization could describe what success looked like without interpretation. One owner per outcome, with real authority and real accountability. A biweekly scorecard review, not to punish, just to see. Progress was visible. Obstacles named. Momentum tracked where people could watch it move.

We also introduced a definition of "done" standard. Every initiative needed a clear endpoint: what 'done' looks like and how the team would know they'd reached it.

This sounds basic. For her, it was revolutionary, because she had been operating on the assumption that smart people would figure out the finish line. Smart people can, but they won't if they don't trust that the finish line will still be there when they arrive.

Then we addressed the hardest behavior: rescuing.

She had a habit of stepping in at the last minute when work wasn't meeting her standard. She'd take over a project, rewrite a deliverable, or redirect a team's approach literally the day before a deadline. It felt helpful, and at times the work got better, but it taught the organization something insidious: standards are optional because the leader will fix it anyway. Why stretch for excellence when someone will swoop in and override your judgment at the eleventh hour?

We replaced rescuing with accountability. When work didn't meet the standard, she named the gap clearly, provided support, and held the person responsible for closing it. Not with punishment. With expectation. The difference between rescuing and developing is whether you take the problem back or keep it with the person who needs to grow.

Over the following 90 days, the shift was slow at first, then consistent, and by the end unmistakable. Engagement improved because teams saw follow-through becoming dependable. People started investing again, with real effort, not hedged effort, because they believed the direction would hold long enough for their work to matter. Performance improved because priorities became real and progress became visible. Her credibility rose, not because she had better ideas, she'd always had those, but because the system began finishing what it started.

"I always thought I had to have all the answers. Now I realize it's about having a reliable system in place to find the answers and for me to follow through."

Competence isn't what you know. It's what the organization can count on you to deliver. When that delivery becomes inconsistent, all the brilliance in the world won't keep trust intact.

Story 6.2—The Delegation Bottleneck

The leader cared about quality. That was the root of everything, both the strength and the fracture.

He had built his reputation on getting things right. Every deliverable that left his desk was polished. Every decision he made had been thoroughly considered. His standards were high, and for most of his career, those standards had been an asset. People trusted him because the work was always excellent.

The problem was that the work was always excellent because he touched everything.

When I started working with him, I could see the bottleneck before anyone described it. The signs were everywhere. Teams waited for approval on decisions they could have made themselves. Good people sat idle while their proposals moved through a review process that had one gate and one gatekeeper. His calendar was a wall of back-to-back meetings, each one a decision that needed his input before anything could move.

"I don't understand why I'm so exhausted," he told me. "I've delegated. I tell people to take ownership."

I asked a few simple questions. "When your team takes ownership and the outcome doesn't match your standard, what happens?" When someone makes a decision you wouldn't have made, how long before you step in? When a deliverable lands at 85 percent of your standard, do you coach it forward or redo it yourself?"

The answer came after a long pause: "I'll fix it."

There it was.

He had delegated the tasks but not the authority. People were given work to do, but the decision rights stayed with him. And every time he overrode a decision or revised an output, he sent a message louder than any delegation memo: your judgment isn't trusted here.

The team had adapted accordingly. They stopped thinking ahead because decisions wouldn't move until he touched them. They stopped taking initiative because initiative was expensive; it cost them time they'd never get back when he revised their work.

Engagement decreased because autonomy had disappeared. Performance slowed because he had become the system's narrowest point. Everything flowed through one person, and one person only has so many hours.

The cost wasn't just organizational. It was personal. He was burning out, not because he had too much work, but because he'd created a system where he was the only path for work to move along. Every decision, every deliverable, every approval ran through his desk. He was working harder than anyone in the building. His effort wasn't multiplying through the organization the way a leader's effort should.

We built a decision rights map. A simple document, but one that required him to make difficult choices about where to release control. We defined five categories:

1. decisions that belong fully to the leader, including strategic direction, resource allocation, and organizational commitments;
2. decisions that belong fully to the team with no approval needed;
3. decisions that require consultation before finalizing;

4. decisions where the team recommends and the leader decides;
5. decisions that get escalated only when a defined threshold is crossed.

The map itself was straightforward. Living by it was not.

The first time a team member made a decision in the "team authority" category and the outcome wasn't what he would have chosen, we had our first of several coaching moments. New patterns were forming, and he was struggling to learn how to truly delegate. His instinct was to make corrections. My question: "Was the outcome acceptable? Not perfect, but acceptable."

"Yes, but—"

"Then leave it. And tell them what they did well."

That was the discipline that changed everything. He had to learn the difference between his standard and the minimum viable standard. Some decisions need to be excellent. Many decisions need to be good enough and fast. When a leader holds every decision to their personal standard of excellence, they don't raise the organization's quality. They lower its speed, its ownership, and its confidence.

We also worked on building a new reflex. When someone brought a problem to his desk, instead of solving it, he asked, "What do you recommend?" and "What would it take for you to own this decision next time?"

That second question is the one that builds organizational competence over time. It shifts the conversation from "give me the answer" to "give me the authority." And it teaches the leader to invest in capacity rather than control.

Over the next four months, his behavior had shifted visibly, and the results followed.

Engagement rose because people regained ownership. They stopped waiting and started acting, not recklessly, but with the clarity of knowing what was theirs to decide. Performance improved because work moved without waiting for one person. Decisions happened faster. Cycle times shortened. And his workload decreased, not because he was doing less, but because the system had learned to carry more.

"I thought I was protecting quality. I was actually preventing growth, both mine and theirs."

Leaders don't burn out because they have too much work. They burn out because they've become the only path for work to move. And when you're the bottleneck, your high standards don't elevate the organization. They choke it.

Story 6.3—The CEO Who Earned It All and Couldn't Let Go

He had earned every promotion he had ever received. That was the first thing you needed to know about him. It was also the root of the problem.

From his first role in operations to his first VP title to the CEO seat he now occupied, he had succeeded by outworking and outthinking everyone around him. He was not the kind of leader who delegated because he lacked the ability to do the work himself. He was the kind of leader who had done every job below him and had done it all very well. He had never been given a reason to believe anyone else could do it as well as he could.

He was right for most of his career. And then he was promoted into a role where that certainty became the problem.

When he came to me, the presenting issue was exhaustion. Seventy-hour weeks. A calendar that started at six in the morning and almost never ended before nine at night, with little downtime in between. He described it the way high performers often do, not as a complaint but as evidence of commitment. This is what the work requires.

I asked him a different question: what was his team doing while he was doing all of it?

The silence that followed was longer than he expected.

Here is what the data showed when we mapped his week against his team's. Decisions that should have taken hours were taking days because they required his approval. Projects that should have been owned by his directors were being partially executed and then quietly parked while they waited for his input. His calendar was full. His team's calendars had gaps, and those gaps were filled not with forward momentum but with waiting.

Before I shared any of that with him, I spent time with his team in one-on-ones. What I heard was not anger. It was something more instructive. They liked him. They respected what he had built and admired how hard he worked. But over time, they had learned to manage around him rather than through him. When a decision needed to move and he was unavailable, they found ways to reframe it so it no longer required his sign-off. When a project needed his energy and he was stretched thin, they scoped it down to what could move without him. They were not staging a quiet rebellion. They were surviving inside a system that had made his presence a prerequisite for nearly everything.

When I asked what they wanted most, the answer was consistent across every conversation: permission. Not praise. Not more feedback on their thinking. Permission to make calls without running everything up the chain first. They did not want to be managed less. They wanted to be trusted more.

The hardest conversation in our work together was not about his schedule or his delegation habits. It was the moment I named what his team had already done in response to the bottleneck he had become.

They had stopped waiting.

When I said that directly, he went quiet in a different way than he had before. Not the quiet of someone processing information. The quiet of someone who had just understood something they could not un-understand.

"They were not waiting for me," he said. "They had stopped."

That sentence was the turning point. Not because it was devastating, though it was, but because it was precise. He was an operator. He understood systems. And he had just seen clearly, for the first time, what kind of system he had developed.

We rebuilt from that recognition. Not by asking him to lower his standards, which were real and which the organization needed, but by separating his standards from his presence. What did excellence look like in each domain? Who on his team could hold that standard if he defined it clearly and then got out of the way? Where had he confused being involved with being responsible?

The work was structural. Decision rights documented. Approval thresholds raised. A weekly rhythm where his job was to ask questions rather than provide answers. The discipline of staying in the room for the conversation but not interjecting his opinion into the decisions.

As he released control, something else shifted that had nothing to do with the organization. His hours came down. Not all at once, but steadily and visibly. And as they did, something he had not named as a loss until it started returning became clear. He was going home. Not just physically, but actually. He was present at dinner. He was not half-inside a problem while his family talked around him. He told me once, without prompting, that his wife had said he seemed like himself again. He did not elaborate. He did not need to.

The moment I knew the work had taken hold at the organizational level came three months later. His VP of Product had made a significant platform decision, one he would have redirected eighteen months earlier, and he had let it stand. Not because he had given up. Because he had read the recommendation, saw the reasoning, and concluded that his VP's judgment was sound.

Six months after that, a director-level role opened. He promoted from within. The person he chose was someone he would have passed over two years before, not because she lacked ability, but because her style was different from his, and he had once confused different with wrong. He did not pass over her this time. He saw what she could do with room to do it.

The organization did not just move faster after that. It moved in more directions at once because more people had been trusted to move it.

"They stopped waiting for me to fix things," he told me near the end of our work together. "That was the moment I knew it was working."

Story 6.4—The Superintendent Who Couldn't Get Out of Her Own System

A superintendent I worked with had been in the same district for eleven years. She knew every family, every school, and every principal. That depth of knowledge was her greatest asset. It was also, by the time we began working together, the system's greatest liability.

When an internal quarterly review flagged two compliance issues, she was alarmed. But the review report wasn't the issue. It was a symptom.

The real issue was this: eleven years of deep familiarity had replaced documented systems. Critical processes lived in her head, not in any protocol or handoff document that another person could run. When I asked her to walk me through how compliance tracking worked, she described a workflow with no formal owner, no written standard, and no escalation path if she wasn't available.

"I just know how to check it," she told me.

"What happens when you don't?" I asked.

She paused. The audit had answered that question for her.

We spent six weeks doing nothing other than documenting what she knew. Every informal protocol. Every silent standard. Every piece of institutional knowledge that lived in her head. We wrote it down. Assigned owners. Built a quarterly audit process with a checklist she didn't have to run personally.

Three months later, she told me something I've carried into every engagement since:

I thought knowing everything made me valuable.
Now I realize it made everyone else fragile.

That's the competence trap in its purest form. A leader who becomes the system rather than building one doesn't protect the organization. They make it dependent.

Competence is the pillar that turns intention into execution. It is what separates leaders who inspire from leaders who build. A team can tolerate a leader who is occasionally unclear or sometimes inconsistent. It cannot sustain a leader whose systems do not work.

When competence holds, people stop managing around the gaps and start moving toward the work. When it breaks, the most talented people leave first because they have the most options.

Build the systems. Develop the bench. Make the organization capable of delivering without you.

Competence ensures your organization can deliver. But delivery without protecting the people who carry the load creates a different kind of failure, one that shows up in quiet exits and burned-out high performers. That is where Chapter 7 begins.

CHAPTER 7: CARE—PROTECTION, NOT PATERNALISM

"Real care is not about making people comfortable. It's about protecting what they need to do their best work."

—Gearl Loden

Most leaders confuse care with kindness.

They think care means being nice, avoiding hard conversations, protecting people from discomfort, and making people happy. But that's not care. That's conflict avoidance disguised as compassion.

Real care is harder.

Care means protecting what matters, even when protection is uncomfortable.

The Two Forms of Care

Form 1: Emotional Care (Protecting Feelings)

This is what most leaders think of when they hear "Care": being empathetic, listening to concerns, showing appreciation, and creating psychological safety. These matter. But alone, they're insufficient.

Leaders who only practice emotional care often lower standards to avoid disappointing people, delay hard conversations to "protect" feelings, and tolerate poor performance because "they're going through a tough time."

This isn't Care. It's paternalism. It treats people as fragile. It assumes they can't handle truth or accountability.

Form 2: Systemic Care (Protecting Capacity)

This is what actually builds trust: removing unnecessary work, saying "no" to requests that would overload the team, enforcing boundaries around workload and personal time, and addressing underperformers so high performers don't burn out.

Systemic care protects people's capacity to do great work instead of just protecting their comfort.

Test: Are you protecting people's feelings or protecting their ability to succeed sustainably?

How Care Breaks

Care breaks in three predictable ways:

Erosion Pattern 1: Rewarding High Performance with More Work

Leaders see someone doing great work and think: "I need them on this next project." So they keep assigning high-stakes work to high performers. Eventually, high performers burn out or leave. Because opportunity without capacity protection isn't care; it's extraction.

The leader is confused: "I gave them the best opportunities. Why are they leaving?"

The Fix: Before assigning new work, ask: "How's your capacity right now?" If someone's been running at 90% for three months, don't add more. Redistribute existing work first.

Erosion Pattern 2: Lowering Standards to "Be Kind"

Leaders see someone struggling and think, "I'll lower expectations to give them breathing room."

But lowering standards doesn't help anyone. The person gets further behind because they need support, not lower expectations. High performers get resentful because they're covering the gap. The team concludes that standards don't matter.

The Fix: Hold the standard. Provide support.

"The expectation hasn't changed, but here's what I'll do to help you meet it: [specific support]. Can we talk about what you need?"

Erosion Pattern 3: Confusing Kindness with Care

Kindness avoids discomfort.
Care addresses it.

Kindness says, "I know you're going through a tough time. Take all the time you need."

Care says, "I know you're going through a tough time. Here's what we'll adjust. Here's what still needs to happen. Let's figure out how to make both work."

Kindness feels good at the moment. Care builds trust over time.

The Energy Stewardship Model

Care means treating people's energy as a finite resource.

Leaders who don't practice energy stewardship add initiatives without removing work, schedule back-to-back meetings with no recovery time, expect people to be "always on," and normalize working late as dedication. This isn't high performance. It's energy extraction.

Leaders who practice energy stewardship remove one thing before adding another, block calendar time for deep work, model boundaries by not sending emails late into the evening, and track workload as carefully as output.

Strategic Pruning

One of the most important care behaviors is removing work.

Most leaders add initiatives. Few remove them. The result: teams drown in accumulated priorities that no longer matter.

Strategic Pruning asks three questions:

- **What are we doing that we should stop?** Projects that made sense two years ago but don't align with current priorities.
- **What are we doing that someone else could do better, cheaper, or faster?** Work that doesn't require your team's specific expertise.
- **What are we doing that doesn't move the mission forward?** Busywork, legacy processes, and meetings that exist because they always have.

Prune quarterly. Protect capacity.

The line between care and paternalism is one of the most difficult boundaries in leadership. The two scenarios that follow test whether you can protect your people's capacity without enabling dependency and whether you can hold high standards while caring for the humans who carry them.

Care in Practice: Don't Judge the Book

In many leadership transitions, I discovered I wasn't just inheriting a role; I was inheriting an unspoken list of people the organization had already decided were beyond hope.

I refused to accept that at face value. Inheriting someone else's judgment about a person's ceiling is one of the most dangerous shortcuts in leadership. Often the people others had dismissed turned out to be some of the most capable, loyal, and determined professionals I ever worked alongside. Not every one of them. But enough to teach me something I now carry into every transition: you don't know what someone is capable of until you invest in them.

It is remarkable how many people I have worked with who have thrived after being underestimated by the previous administration. And I have built some of my strongest professional relationships with people who interviewed for the same position I was hired for. That dynamic, where someone wanted your job and didn't get it, can feel like a landmine. It isn't. It is an opportunity. If you approach it with care, honesty, and respect, it often becomes the foundation of your most trusted working relationships.

Care in these moments does not require a grand gesture. It requires a genuine conversation, one where you ask what they see, what they have been working to build, and what they need to be able to do their best work. It requires extending the benefit of the doubt before the evidence is fully in, and then paying close attention to the evidence, not the reputation.

Don't judge the book by what the last reader said about it. Open it. Give it a read.

Care in Practice: The Company That Had Everything Except Protection

The company had been a dominant force in its field for over two decades. Then the industry shifted in ways leadership had not anticipated, and the response was too slow and too late. By the time the board acted, the damage was visible. The CEO was removed publicly. Several key leaders followed, some pushed out, and others chose to leave rather than navigate what came next. What remained was a workforce that had been running hard for years trying to recapture something that felt further away with every quarter.

The company paid well. It celebrated wins loudly. It had recognition programs, incentive structures, and benefits that ranked among the best in the sector. From the outside, it looked like an organization that understood how to care for its people. From the inside, it felt like an organization that had confused compensation with care and celebration with protection.

The new CEO had been brought in specifically because the organization needed stabilization, and he had done this kind of work before. What he did not know, not yet, was how wide and how deep the real problem ran.

He found out at his first town hall.

The questions were not hostile. They were direct in the way that questions become when people have been waiting a long time for someone who will actually listen. People asked about training budgets that had been promised and never released. About resources that existed on paper and not in practice. About workloads that had grown through the reorganization without anything being removed. About a culture where working harder had become the only accepted response to a problem, regardless of whether harder was what the problem actually required.

He had expected some of this. He had not expected all of it, and he had not expected it to be so consistent across every level of the organization. The engagement surveys confirmed what the town hall had surfaced. The scores on workload sustainability were the lowest in the company's history, sitting alongside compensation scores that were among the highest. The combination told a precise story. The company had been paying people well to be exhausted and calling it care.

When I sat with him after that first round of data, he was quiet in the way that leaders get when something they believed has just been rearranged. He had inherited a culture built on compensation and celebration, and he had assumed those things were evidence enough that the organization cared for its people. What the data showed him was that his people did not feel protected. They felt spent.

The first structural move was the training and resources budget that had been sitting approved but undeployed. He released it and did not announce it as a gift. He announced it as an overdue obligation, because that is what it was. The money had been there. The decision to withhold it had been a choice, and now reversing it was a choice too; and he said so plainly. Within thirty days, teams that had been asking for tools and development for over a year began receiving them.

The second move came out of a coaching session. A high-profile initiative had been launched with significant internal fanfare before his arrival. It was adding pressure across three divisions without producing the results that had justified it. I asked him what he thought the ultimate act of care would look like at that moment. He sat with the question. Then he said, "I need to suspend that initiative." Not pausing it quietly. Suspending it publicly, with an explanation.

He announced it in a leadership meeting, explained the reasoning, and acknowledged that the organization had been carrying the weight of something that was no longer earning its place on the plate. He did not frame it as a failure of the previous leadership. He framed it as a decision he was making now because protecting the organization's capacity was his responsibility. Removing it was not an admission of failure. It was an act of care.

The third move became a standing discipline. Every direct report had a standing agenda item in their monthly 1:1: workload. What was on the plate, what was sustainable, what needed to come off before anything new was added. He held to it without exception and acted on what he heard.

The organization's response was not immediate celebration. It was, however, relief. There is a difference, and it matters. Celebration is what people do when something good happens. Relief is what people do when something that has been wrong is finally named and addressed. The town halls changed in tone. Not because the problems disappeared but because people believed, for the first time in a long time, that the person at the top understood the difference between paying people and protecting them.

Retention stabilized. The exits slowed. People who had been interviewing quietly stopped. Not because the work became easier but because the environment had signaled something it had not signaled before: that their capacity mattered as much as their output and that the leader at the top would make structural decisions to protect both.

He told me at the end of our work together that the hardest part had not been making the changes. The hardest part had been accepting that the recognition programs and the compensation packages he had inherited had been functioning as a substitute for the harder work of actually protecting people. The company had been celebrating its people while quietly extracting from them. The two things had coexisted long enough that leadership had stopped seeing the contradiction.

Care is not what you pay people. It is not what you celebrate. It is what you build into the system so that people can sustain excellence without burning through themselves to produce it. When those structures are absent, compensation becomes a transaction and celebration becomes noise. And eventually, even the most committed people stop believing that the organization sees them as anything more than output with a bonus attached.

Trust in Action: Two Moments That Test Care

Moment: The Workload That's Unsustainable

Context: You're a senior leader. Your team is drowning. Every time you add a new initiative, people nod in agreement, but nothing gets removed. Burnout is visible. Quality is slipping.

The Trust Test: Do you keep adding and hope people figure it out? Pause to remove work before adding more? Or tell people to "prioritize better"?

Pillars Tested: Care, Clarity, Courage

What Strong Leaders Do: They stop adding and start removing.

"We need to talk about workload. I've been adding initiatives without removing anything, and that's not sustainable. Starting today, we're pausing all new work for 30 days. In that time, we're going to identify what we stop, reduce, or delegate. I'm not asking you to do more with less; I'm asking us to do less, better."

Why This Works: It names the problem directly instead of pretending it's fine. It stops the bleeding immediately, which demonstrates care. It creates a process for pruning, which demonstrates leadership, and it redefines success around quality rather than volume.

The Trust Leak: Leaders who keep adding without removing train people not to take new initiatives seriously. Everything becomes a "priority," which means nothing is.

Moment: The High Performer You're Accidentally Destroying

Context: You're a department head. Your best person, the one who always delivers, just turned in another flawless project. In the team meeting, you publicly praised them. Later that day, you assigned them the next high-stakes project because "you need someone you can count on."

What you didn't see: They've worked late four nights this week. They're covering for two underperformers. They're exhausted; they just said yes again because they always do.

Three months later, they resigned.

The Trust Test: Do you keep assigning work to your most capable people because results matter? Distribute work evenly, even if it means lower-quality outcomes? Or track workload as carefully as you track performance?

Pillars Tested: Care, Competence, Consistency

What Strong Leaders Do: They protect capacity.

Before assigning the next project:

"Before I assign this, I need to check in. You've carried a heavy load lately: the Q3 analysis, the board presentation, and covering for the team gaps we still haven't filled. How's your capacity right now?"

"Here's what I'm worried about: I keep coming to you because you deliver, but I might be overloading you without realizing it. I need you to be sustainable, not just productive. If this project pushes you past sustainability, I need to know now, not when you're burned out."

Why This Works: It names the pattern directly, which shows awareness. It asks instead of assumes, which demonstrates care. It prioritizes sustainability over short-term output, which demonstrates competence. And it makes it safe to say no, which demonstrates character.

The Trust Leak: High performers don't quit jobs. They quit leaders who take their capacity for granted, who reward performance with more work, and who don't notice when "yes" becomes automatic rather than enthusiastic. Every time you overload a high performer without checking capacity, you make a trust withdrawal. Eventually, the account empties.

The Hidden Pattern: Leaders fall into this trap because high performers don't complain often, so you don't see the load. Assigning work to them feels efficient, so you don't question it. They keep delivering, so you assume they're fine. But "not complaining" doesn't mean "not drowning."

The Competence + Care Integration: This moment tests whether you've built a system that distributes work based on capacity, not just capability; that tracks workload as a metric, not just output; and that develops bench strength instead of relying on heroics. Competence says, "I need a system that works without burning out my best people." Care says, "I need to protect the people who make everything else possible." Both must be true.

The Real Conversation (When You've Already Overloaded Them)

"I need to acknowledge something. I've overloaded you. I've done it repeatedly, and I didn't check capacity before adding on more. That's not fair to you, and it's not sustainable for the team. Here's what I'm changing: I'm redistributing specific projects to other team members. And I'm meeting with you monthly to review workload before I assign anything new. It's me fixing a system that was breaking you."

Why This Works: It owns the mistake, which demonstrates character. It acts immediately, which demonstrates urgency. It changes the system, which demonstrates competence. It also protects going forward, which demonstrates care.

Prevention Strategy: Monthly Workload Check

Five minutes per person:

"On a scale of 1–10, how sustainable is your workload right now? One means drowning. Five means at capacity but managing. Ten means you could take more. If you're below 5, what needs to come off your plate?"

Track this. If someone's been below 5 for two months straight, you have a distribution problem, not a performance problem."

The Consistency Test: Do you protect high performers' capacity as consistently as you expect high performance? If not, you're making withdrawals without deposits.

Your System Check:

- *Who on your team is running at an unsustainable capacity right now?*
- *What will you remove from their plate in the next 48 hours?*

These scenarios test your instincts. However, the deepest care failures aren't about single decisions; they're about patterns that slowly extract more from people than they return. The following stories show what happens when leaders confuse demanding more with caring well.

LEADERSHIP IN PRACTICE: CARE

Story 7.1—High Standards Without Protection

The results were strong. That was the first thing anyone would tell you about this team.

Deadlines were met. Projects shipped. The numbers looked good from every angle leadership cared to measure. The team leader had built a culture of discipline and execution, and by most external standards, her model was working.

So when she reached out to me, I was curious about what she thought needed fixing.

"I'm losing people," she said. "And I don't understand why. The team is performing. We're hitting targets. We have great incentives and benefits. We have celebrations. Between the incentives, the celebrations, and the results, I honestly thought we'd built something people wouldn't want to leave."

And she had.

What she hadn't counted on was that people didn't want to be on a team that was winning at their expense.

I wanted to understand why they were leaving. So I spent time with the team. What I found wasn't dysfunction, it was erosion. The kind that doesn't show up in quarterly metrics but lives in the faces of people who have been running at full speed for too long without anyone acknowledging the cost.

The team was tired. Not the ordinary tiredness that follows a hard sprint, but the deep tiredness that comes from living in a permanent state of urgency. Every week, there was a fire. Every project had an accelerated timeline. Every expectation was calibrated to the ceiling, and recovery was treated as a luxury the organization couldn't afford.

People were guarded. Conversations stayed surface-level, professional, and efficient but were drained of the candor that fuels real collaboration. Team members had become transactional. They did what was asked, delivered what was required, and saved their real energy for life outside of work, not because they had stopped caring, but because caring had become a liability in an environment that only rewarded output.

She interpreted the guardedness as professionalism. After digging in, I saw it for what it was: self-protection.

One conversation told me everything I needed to know. A team member, someone she considered a top performer, said quietly: "I can't remember the last time someone asked how I was doing without it turning into more work."

This team had weathered a post-COVID reorganization, a full retraining cycle, and now the job shifts that came with adopting AI. Each wave came with new expectations but no new space to absorb them. The top performer's statement wasn't just one of frustration. It was the sound of care becoming invisible.

The leader cared. I did not doubt that. She worked as hard as anyone. She sacrificed her own time. She championed her team in rooms the team never saw. But care that isn't visible to the people who need it doesn't count. Not because the intent doesn't matter, but because the intent doesn't land. Leadership isn't graded on intent.

When I said that to her directly, she was quiet for a moment. Then she said, "I've been working harder than anyone on this team. How is that not visible?" I told her that working hard and protecting people are not the same thing. She knew it was true before I finished the sentence.

We reframed care as protection, not as softness, not as lowering standards, but as building the structural conditions that allow people to sustain excellence without breaking.

She began doing three things consistently:

First, she named the workload reality out loud. Not pretending capacity was infinite. Not celebrating the grind. Just honest acknowledgment: "This is a heavy period. I see it. And I need your help figuring out what to do about it." Then she did something leaders often skip: she listened. She asked the team what was draining them most, what felt unnecessary, and what they would change if they had the authority. She didn't act on all of it, but she acted on enough of it that people knew their input had weight. That alone changed the temperature in the room, because when a leader names the weight and then moves based on what the team sees, people stop carrying it in silence.

Second, she adopted a discipline I consider non-negotiable in high-performance cultures: remove one burden when you add a new demand. If a new initiative was launched, something else came off the plate. Not next quarter. Now. This forced her to confront a truth she'd been avoiding: she had been adding expectations for months without subtracting any, and the team had been absorbing the accumulation without complaint because complaining wasn't safe.

Third, she normalized recovery as a performance strategy. Not a perk. Not a reward for hitting a milestone. A strategy. She began talking about sustainability the same way she talked about execution, as a discipline required for long-term results. Rest wasn't the absence of work. It was the investment that made work renewable. She even modeled this by doing something uncharacteristic: unplugging and taking a few days off.

We also installed what I call "truth moments" in team meetings. One question, asked weekly at first: "Where are we overloading the system right now?" The first time she asked, the room was silent. The second time, one person spoke up tentatively. By the fourth week, the team was having the most honest conversations they'd had in a year. Once that became the norm, she moved it to monthly. The question didn't need to be weekly anymore because her consistency had created permission.

After several months of consistent communication and visible care, the shift was visible to everyone.

Engagement increased because people felt seen and protected. Not coddled. Protected. There's a vast difference. Coddling means the leader removes difficulty. "Protected" means the leader ensures that difficulty doesn't become damage. The team began taking initiative again, not out of fear of falling short but out of genuine belief that their effort would be met with support, not just more expectations.

Performance improved because energy returned. People who had been running on fumes found reserves they'd forgotten they had. Not because the workload decreased dramatically, but because the environment had signaled that their well-being was part of the system.

Stay interviews revealed that the turnover risk had faded. The people who'd been considering leaving recognized something had changed structurally, and she was building an environment they wanted to stay in.

Care isn't kindness. It's designing an environment where people can sustain excellence. And when leaders confuse care with softness, they build cultures that perform brilliantly until they don't. And the collapse, when it comes, feels sudden to everyone except the people who lived through the slow burn.

Story 7.2—The Leader Who Confused "Nice" With Care

Everyone liked this leader. That was part of the problem.

He was warm, approachable, and supportive. The kind of leader who remembered your birthday, asked about your family, and made time for you even when his schedule was full.

People enjoyed working for him. If you'd surveyed the team on whether their leader cared, the scores would have been high, and yet the team was slowly unraveling.

The signal wasn't in his behavior. It was in everyone else's. Strong performers were quietly carrying extra weight. Mediocre performance was lingering in plain sight. The team had an unspoken hierarchy, not based on title or talent, but on who was willing to absorb the load that under-performers left behind.

He saw it. He wasn't blind, but he didn't act on it. Acting on it would mean having hard conversations that didn't fit his leadership identity.

He'd built his reputation on being the leader who cared. Somewhere along the way, "caring" had become synonymous with "not confronting."

When I asked him where that belief came from, he did not have to think long. Earlier in his career he had worked for a leader who ran on fear. Criticism was public. Standards were enforced through humiliation. People performed not because they believed in the work but because they were afraid of what happened when they did not. He had watched that leader break people, and he had made a quiet promise to himself that he would never be the reason someone dreaded coming to work.

That promise was honorable. The problem was what it had become. Over time, the promise not to harm had quietly expanded into a promise not to confront, and somewhere in that slow drift, caring and accountability had come to feel like opposites. They were not. But he had lived inside that equation long enough that it felt true.

When I named it directly, that his avoidance was not protecting his team but costing them, he pushed back. He listed the things he did. The birthday cards. The flexibility he offered when people had hard weeks. The time he spent listening. He was not wrong about any of it. The care was real. What I asked him to see was that his people who were carrying the extra load did not experience any of those gestures as protection. They experienced them as evidence that the standard would never be enforced. That they were on their own.

The result was a team where kindness had become a shield against accountability. The people paying the price weren't the underperformers. It was the strong ones, the people doing the extra work, holding the extra standard, and compensating silently for the gaps he refused to name.

In a one-on-one with a longtime high performer, she told me, "My leader is a great guy, and I know he cares about me. I do. But if he really cared, he'd stop having me do half of someone else's job on top of mine. It's not right. And I'm tired of pretending it is."

That distinction, between caring about someone and caring enough to act, is the difference between goodwill and leadership.

The intervention wasn't about making him harsh. It was about helping him understand that care without accountability isn't care. It's avoidance, and the team was paying for the avoidance every day.

The missing piece wasn't courage. He had that. What he lacked was a repeatable way to deliver hard truth without it feeling like an attack. A script built for clarity, not comfort. He practiced five sentences until they became natural:

"Here's the standard. Here's what I'm seeing. Here's what has to change. Here's the support I'll provide. Here's the timeline."

Five sentences. No ambiguity. No attack on character. No emotional escalation. Just a clear description of reality, expectation, and support.

It was easy for him to identify who the lower performers were. That was never the problem. The real coaching was helping him see that authentic care requires leading with standards too, that avoiding hard conversations wasn't kindness. It was avoidance disguised as wearing a kind face.

The first conversation was the hardest. He almost backed out twice. He kept finding reasons to delay: "Maybe I should give them one more week." "Maybe I'm being too hard." I reminded him of something he already knew but didn't want to face: every week he delayed, the strong performers carried more weight, and the message to the entire team was that performance standards were negotiable.

He held the conversation. It was brief, direct, and respectful. The person on the receiving end wasn't blindsided; they'd sensed the gap themselves. What they needed wasn't another graceful pass. They needed to know the expectation was real and that support was available.

Over time, and through consistent coaching conversations, engagement rose because strong performers felt protected. The people carrying the team saw evidence that he would hold the standard, not just for the people who were already meeting it, but especially for those who weren't. That's a trust deposit that compounds.

Performance improved because standards became real rather than theoretical. The underperforming team member either rose to meet the standard with coaching and support or moved on. Either outcome was healthier than the status quo.

As a result, his relationships actually strengthened. This is the part that surprises leaders who avoid hard conversations: people don't trust you less when you hold them accountable with dignity. They trust you more. Because accountability with clarity and support says, "I believe you can do this, and I won't let you settle for less."

His own self-image shifted, too. He stopped defining care as the absence of discomfort and started defining it as the willingness to protect what matters, including the team's right to be led with honesty, clarity, and high expectations, in addition to the warmth he naturally brought to the table. He told me, "I was managing my own discomfort and calling it compassion. I thought I was being a good leader by not making people uncomfortable. Turns out I was just making the wrong people comfortable."

Care without accountability isn't care. It's avoidance that the team pays for. The longer a leader lets that debt accumulate, the more it costs the people who can least afford it.

Story 7.3—The Leader Who Held the Line

When a new CEO inherited a team with a toxic culture, years of leadership turnover, and performance decline, the pressure was immediate. Several board members wanted terminations. Swift ones. They wanted her to send a signal in the first thirty days that the old way was over.

At first, her instinct was to do the same.

She told me that during our early sessions. She was not immune to the pressure. There was a specific leader on her team, someone who had been part of the dysfunction for years, who had become a symbol of everything that needed to change. The board wanted him gone. Several of her direct reports wanted him gone. There were days she wanted him gone. It would have been easy. It would have felt decisive, and it would have told the organization something about who she was.

She held. Not because she was certain she was right, but because she understood something she had seen go wrong before: accountability without dignity creates fear, and fear destroys the very capacity you need to rebuild. An organization that watches its new CEO make a swift example of someone does not conclude that standards have arrived. It concludes that safety has left. Those are not the same thing, and she knew the difference.

So she chose the harder path, and she chose it while knowing what it could cost her personally. If the approach did not produce results fast enough, if the board lost patience before the culture shifted, she would be next. Her credibility was the collateral on a bet that care and accountability could coexist.

She began with conversations. Every leader on her team received a direct performance discussion within the first sixty days. Not a warning. Not a probationary review. A clarity session. "Here is what I see. Here is what the role requires. Here is the support I will provide. Here is the timeline." No ambiguity, no softening, and no public spectacle.

The moment I think about most when I tell this story happened in one of those early conversations. A leader sat across from her who had survived each leadership change and reorganization, each new regime change, by staying small, staying quiet, and giving just enough to avoid being the first name on any list. He had learned, through years of watching what happened to people who raised their hands or spoke plainly, that the safest posture was invisibility. He came into that room braced for the version of the conversation he had learned to expect.

Instead, she asked him what he needed to do his best work.

He did not answer right away. The question landed differently than he expected. This was early in her tenure, and the organization was still watching to see whether her approach was real or performed. He looked at her for a moment, recalibrating.

She asked it because she meant it, and then she acted on what he said.

The word spread the way words always spread in organizations that have been starved of honest leadership. Not through announcements or all-hands meetings. Through hallways and one-on-ones and the particular way people talk when they are trying to decide whether to trust something new. What people said was not that she was kind. What they said was that she was real. That the conversation had been hard and she had not flinched, and she still asked what they needed. That combination, high standards and genuine investment, was not something this organization had seen together before.

Some leaders rose to meet what she asked. Others recognized the clarity for what it was and chose to leave. A few were exited, directly and respectfully, including eventually the leader the board had wanted gone in the first thirty days. She exited him on her timeline, not theirs, after she had given him the opportunity the role required and he had shown her what she needed to know. When it happened, nobody was surprised. Nobody felt it was unfair. The process had been visible enough that the outcome was simply the conclusion of something everyone had already understood.

Within eighteen months, the company had its strongest leadership bench in a decade. But what she built did not stop at the cabinet table. When directors and middle managers saw that accountability came with investment rather than political maneuvering, they began leading their teams the same way. Honest conversations replaced defensive posturing. People who had spent years keeping their heads down started raising their hands. A quiet confidence replaced the chronic distrust that had defined the culture for years.

And the board took notice. The members who had pushed for swift terminations in her first weeks watched the results build over those eighteen months. The culture data improved. Performance numbers followed. The people they had wanted removed were either leading differently or had been exited through a process nobody could criticize. What she had asked them to trust early on, when the evidence was thin and the risk was real, had produced something none of the previous approaches had. She had not just turned the organization around. She had built something the board could finally stand behind.

None of it happened because she was nice. It happened because she understood that care is not the opposite of standards. It is what makes standards something people want to reach rather than simply endure.

The company did not transform because she lowered the bar. It transformed because she held it steady and gave people a reason to believe that reaching it was worth the effort.

That is the difference between making people comfortable and making people capable. And when that distinction takes root in a single leader's decisions, it has a way of rewriting the story of an entire organization.

CHAPTER 8: CLARITY—TRUTH FASTER THAN RUMOR

Most leaders think they're clearer than they are. When leaders are clear, people know what success looks like, what's changing and what isn't, what's negotiable and what's not. When leaders are unclear, people create their own interpretation, and those interpretations are rarely generous.

Ambiguity doesn't just create confusion.
It multiplies anxiety.

"Clarity isn't about having all the answers. It's about making sure your people never have to guess at the ones that matter." —Gearl Loden

The Ambiguity Problem

Humans are meaning-making machines. When information is incomplete, we automatically fill in the gaps with assumptions shaped by experience, current anxiety, and worst-case scenarios.

A leader says, "We're exploring some changes to the team structure."

What people hear: layoffs are coming. I'm getting reassigned. Leadership doesn't know what they are doing.

What the leader meant: we might shift two people to a new project.

Ambiguity left a gap, and speculation filled it before the leader had a chance to explain.

What Clarity Actually Means

Clarity is not saying everything you know. It's not over-explaining to avoid every possible question, and it's certainly not being blunt to the point of cruelty.

Clarity is naming what's actually happening without softening it into something unrecognizable.

The test: after a conversation with you, can the other person repeat back what you said in their own words? If not, you weren't clear.

The Three Levels of Clarity

Level 1: Clarity of Situation

What's happening right now?

Unclear leaders soften bad news, speak in abstractions, and avoid naming problems directly. They say things like "we're exploring optimization opportunities" when they mean layoffs, "there are some concerns" when they mean a specific problem needs fixing, and "we need to be more strategic" when they haven't defined what strategic means.

Clear leaders name reality without soft framing. They state problems directly: "Revenue is down 15%." "Client retention is the issue." "We're cutting three positions." The language is concrete because clarity requires it.

Level 2: Clarity of Expectation

What does success look like?

Unclear leaders use vague goals like "improve customer satisfaction," speak in generalities like "be more proactive," and leave standards undefined with phrases like "do your best." These statements feel like direction, but they're not. They're ambiguity dressed as delegation.

Clear leaders define observable outcomes: “Reduce response time to under 24 hours.” They specify behaviors: “Bring me issues within 48 hours of discovery.” They state measurable standards: “Attendance at 95% or above.” When success is defined in terms that people can see, people can actually achieve it.

Level 3: Clarity of Decision

What’s decided, and what’s still open?

Unclear leaders present decisions as discussions, creating false hope. They present discussions as decisions, shutting down input. They leave the status ambiguous with phrases like "we're thinking about it," telling people nothing about whether their voice matters in the outcome.

Clear leaders name what’s decided: “This decision is final.” They name what’s still open: “I need your input on X before deciding.” And they communicate the timeline: “A decision will be made by Friday.” When people know the status of a decision, they stop wasting energy trying to figure out whether to lobby, comply, or wait.

How Clarity Breaks

Clarity breaks in three predictable ways:

Erosion Pattern 1: Softening Truth to Avoid Discomfort

Leaders soften bad news with good intentions, but softening creates confusion. People spend energy decoding what was meant instead of responding to reality.

“We’re right-sizing the organization” means layoffs. “We’re pausing investment in this area” means it’s dead. “We’re exploring all options” means we don’t know what to do.

The Fix: Say what you mean directly. “We’re eliminating three positions. Here’s why. Here’s the timeline. Here’s what this means for the rest of the team.”

Erosion Pattern 2: Leaving Interpretation to Others

Leaders say things like "Make this a priority," "Improve performance," and "Be more strategic." These statements feel clear to the leader because they know what they mean, but they're ambiguous to the listener.

The Fix: Test for clarity by asking, "Can you repeat back what success looks like?" If they can't, you weren't clear.

Erosion Pattern 3: Talking Around the Problem

Leaders avoid naming uncomfortable truths. Instead of "your performance isn't meeting expectations," they say, "let's talk about development opportunities." Instead of "this project failed," they say "we're learning from this experience." Instead of "we disagree," they say "let's align our thinking." This feels kind, but it's not. It's confusing.

The Fix: Name what's true, even if it's uncomfortable. "Your performance isn't meeting expectations. Here's the gap. Here's what needs to change. Here's the timeline."

The Clarity Test

After any conversation, meeting, or message, ask yourself three questions.

1. Can they repeat it back? For example, if they had to explain your message to someone else, could they do it accurately?
2. Is there only one interpretation, or could your message be read three different ways?
3. And do they know what success looks like, in observable, measurable terms?

If you can't answer "yes" to all three, you aren't clear.

Clarity Under Pressure: The Coast Guard Standard

The U.S. Coast Guard operates in life-or-death situations where miscommunication kills. Their communication standard: "Brief, clear, and confirms understanding."

Every radio transmission follows this pattern: state the message, require the listener to repeat it back, and confirm or correct. "Vessel in distress at coordinates 40.7N, 74.0W. Repeat back." "Coordinates 40.7N, 74.0W confirmed." "Correct. Proceed."

No ambiguity. No assumptions. When lives depend on communication, clarity isn't optional. The same principle applies to leadership. When execution depends on communication, clarity isn't optional.

Clarity vs. Completeness

Leaders often confuse clarity with completeness. Completeness can obscure clarity.

Unclear (complete but confusing): "As you know, market dynamics have shifted significantly over the past quarter, driven by a combination of factors including inflation, supply chain disruptions, and changing consumer preferences, which has led us to reevaluate our strategic positioning across multiple product lines, and after extensive analysis and consultation with key stakeholders, we've determined that the optimal path forward requires us to reallocate resources away from the legacy platform toward emerging opportunities in the digital space, which means we'll be discontinuing support for Version 2.0 effective Q2."

Clear (concise and direct): "We're discontinuing Version 2.0 in Q2. Why: The market has shifted to digital. Customer demand for our legacy platform dropped 40%. Resources will be redirected to our new platform. Timeline: End of support: June 30. Questions?"

Both say the same thing. One is clear. One is exhausting.

Clarity feels simple until you're the one who has to deliver the truth that people don't want to hear, or making a call when the data is incomplete. The two scenarios that follow test your clarity under those real conditions.

Clarity in Practice: More Channels, Same Gap

We have more ways to communicate than at any point in history, with email, text, video, apps, town halls, newsletters, one-on-ones, and all-staff meetings. And leaders still hear it: "I didn't know." "Nobody told me." "I wasn't sure what that meant." More communication channels have not closed the clarity gap. If anything, they have made it easier for important messages to get lost in the noise.

A leader managing a crisis processes information differently than when operations are stable. An operations officer navigating a personnel situation needs something different than a weekly update email. I learned early to stop asking how I preferred to send the message and start asking how my people needed to receive it. Ask them directly; they will tell you. Keep asking, because those needs will shift as your organization and culture evolve. Their answers will tell you more than any survey.

When I have a critical message to deliver, or when I detect that clarity is leaking, that the rumor mill is running faster than my communication, I choose presence first. Face-to-face when possible. A video message when distance or schedules require it, not a polished production but something where people can hear your voice, see your face, and know there is a human being behind the words. That alone changes how the message lands.

Feedback loops matter as much as the message itself. I have built in regular checkpoints across multiple stakeholder groups, not to ask, "Did you get my email?" but to ask, "What are you hearing out there? What is still unclear? What question keeps coming up that I have not answered?" That is where the real clarity work happens. You do not find out that clarity is missing by sending more messages. You find out by creating enough trust that people will tell you when they are confused.

Never give up on communicating. Keep asking how your people need to hear it. Keep adjusting until understanding is actually present.

Trust in Action: Two Moments That Test Clarity

Moment: When the Right Call Is the Unpopular One

Context: You're a hospital administrator shifting resources from a well-regarded and popular wellness program to expand mental health outpatient services. The community need is undeniable. The data support the decision. But it means reducing investment in a program people love and staff have built with genuine pride. You're confident in the long-term impact. In the short term, it's going to create real pain.

The Trust Test: Do you announce it as a done deal and move forward? Do you explain the rationale and invite questions, even knowing some will disagree? Or do you soften the message to avoid the resistance you know is coming?

Pillars Tested: Clarity, Courage, Communication

What Strong Leaders Do: They explain the trade-off precisely and uphold the decision.

"We're reallocating resources from the wellness program to expand our mental health outpatient services. I know this is hard. That program has served our community well, and many of you have built something you're proud of.

Here's why we're making this call: the mental health need in this community is significant and growing, and we have both the responsibility and the opportunity to meet it. This isn't a judgment on what the wellness program has accomplished. It's a decision about where our limited resources will have the greatest impact for the people who need us most.

I'm not asking you to agree with this. I'm asking you to understand it. And if you have concerns, I want to hear them."

Why This Works: It names what's being lost, which acknowledges the human cost. It explains the reasoning clearly, which respects the team's intelligence. It invites dissent without reopening the decision, which signals genuine clarity rather than decree. And it holds the line, which is what leadership requires.

The Trust Leak: Leaders who soften hard truths to avoid resistance create confusion instead of clarity. People don't need leaders who manage their feelings. They need leaders who tell them the truth about hard trade-offs and trust them to handle it.

Moment: The Feedback You Don't Want to Hear

Context: You're a director who just received 360-degree feedback. One theme is clear: your team feels like you don't listen. You think you listen fine; they just don't always like your decisions.

The Trust Test: Do you dismiss it as a misunderstanding? Do you explore what "not listening" actually means to them? Or acknowledge it defensively and move on?

Pillars Tested: Clarity, Character, Care

What Strong Leaders Do: They ask clarifying questions without defending.

"The feedback said I don't listen well. I want to understand that better. What does not listening look like to you? Do you feel like I am not paying attention? That I seem to have already decided before you speak? Is it that I don't change my mind? I need specifics so I can address the right thing."

Why This Works: It doesn't dismiss the feedback, which shows respect. It asks for specifics, which shows genuine curiosity. And it doesn't defend or justify, which creates safety for the person giving input.

The Trust Leak: Leaders who dismiss feedback as "misunderstanding" lose access to truth. Teams stop offering it.

Your System Check:

- *Think about the last message you sent to your team through email, Slack, or an official announcement. Could someone repeat what you said in their own words?*
- *If you're not sure, that's your answer. What will you clarify in the next 24 hours?*

Those scenarios test your clarity under pressure. But keep in mind that the most damaging clarity failures aren't about crisis communication; they're about the everyday ambiguity that leaders mistake for strategic flexibility. The following stories expose that pattern.

LEADERSHIP IN PRACTICE: CLARITY

Story 8.1—Ambiguity as Strategy

The leader believed she was being strategic. What she was actually being was evasive, and she didn't know the difference.

Her reasoning made sense from the inside. By staying vague on priorities, she kept options open. By avoiding a clear ranking of initiatives, she prevented anyone from feeling dismissed. By keeping the language broad, she preserved flexibility to pivot as conditions changed.

From her perspective, ambiguity was agility.

From the team's perspective, ambiguity was a lack of purpose, direction, and alignment.

In every conversation I had with her direct reports, capable and committed people, I heard the same underlying question phrased a dozen different ways: "What are we actually supposed to be doing?"

Not because they lacked work. They had plenty. But they couldn't tell which work mattered most. They couldn't tell which projects had leadership's genuine backing and which were alive only because no one had officially killed them. They were making daily decisions about where to invest their time and energy, and they were making those decisions based on guesswork because she hadn't given them anything more solid to work with.

The cost was everywhere. Teams pursued competing priorities and didn't discover the conflict until resources collided. Rework was chronic, with people building toward one interpretation of the direction only to discover the leader meant something different. Engagement dropped because guessing is exhausting. It's not just mentally draining; it's demoralizing. When people have to guess what matters, they eventually stop caring whether they guess right.

She saw the symptoms, the misalignment, the rework, and the slow execution and interpreted them as a performance problem. "I need sharper people," she told me.

"You don't need sharper people," I said. "Your people need direction, clarity, structure, and alignment; and that starts with you, not them."

That wasn't what she wanted to hear, but it was what she needed to hear. And to her credit, she didn't argue. She sat with it. That's where real leadership growth begins, not in the moment you hear the truth, but in what you do after you've had time to let it settle.

That honesty opened the door.

We built clarity as a discipline, not a one-time exercise in strategic planning, but a repeatable practice she would run consistently. Three things, named out loud, every time. The top priorities, no more than three, with clear criteria for why they'd been chosen. The trade-offs, what was being deprioritized, and why. And what would not be pursued right now.

That "what we are not doing" statement was the hardest one for her to make. It meant closing doors. It meant disappointing people who'd been investing in initiatives that weren't going to be resourced. It meant absorbing the discomfort of saying "no" instead of distributing the discomfort of ambiguity across the entire organization.

We also introduced decision-rights clarity: who decides, who advises, and who executes. Because even when priorities are clear, if people don't know who owns the decision, they default to either waiting for permission or acting and hoping they have authority. Both outcomes waste time and erode confidence.

Over the following 90 days, new patterns formed: clarity checks, coaching conversations, employee feedback loops, and the discipline of monitoring and adjusting as the work revealed what planning couldn't.

Alignment and engagement improved because people had clarity, authority, and direction. There is a visible change in an organization when people shift from "I think this might be what they want" to "I know what we're doing and why." Energy that was being burned on interpretation got redirected to execution.

Performance improved because the organization was focused. When everything is a priority, nothing is. When three things are the priority, teams build momentum. Rework dropped. People were finally building toward a common direction instead of correcting misalignment.

She felt less pressure, which surprised her. She'd assumed that being specific would create more conflict and more pushback from the people whose projects didn't make the cut. What actually happened was the opposite. The conflict decreased because clarity removed the political ambiguity that had been fueling it. When people know the priorities and the reasoning, they may not agree; but they stop lobbying in the shadows.

What she carried forward was this: ambiguity isn't a strategy. It's a cost, and it always gets passed down. Every decision you delay, your team absorbs. Every direction you refuse to commit to, they work around. And they know. They may never say it directly, but they know the difference between a leader who's deciding and a leader who's drifting. One builds trust. The other quietly erodes it.

Story 8.2—Data Without Signal

The Monday morning meeting had been running for ninety minutes, and nothing had been decided. The CEO had called it to address a critical budget realignment. Three operations directors were in the room. Two senior vice presidents. A CFO. Everyone had data. Nobody had clarity. The meeting ended with a follow-up meeting.

The leadership team had more information than they could use. That was the problem.

Dashboards everywhere. Metrics for every function. Weekly reports that ran fifteen to twenty pages. Monthly reviews that consumed entire days. The organization was drowning in data, and the leader was convinced that more data meant better decisions.

When I started working with this team, the meetings weren't hostile; nobody was shouting. But they were adversarial in a quieter way. Every metric had become a weapon. Department leaders cited favorable data to justify their approach and questioned any number that challenged them. The same data set got interpreted three different ways in the same meeting, and every interpretation conveniently served the person presenting it.

Engagement had dropped because the system felt political. People learned to lead with their metrics, not their insights. Meetings became performances where the goal was to look good on paper rather than surface the truth. The most important conversations happened in the parking lot after the meeting, not in the room where decisions were made.

Performance had stagnated. Not because the organization lacked talent or drive, but because the energy that should have been spent improving was being spent arguing about which numbers told the real story.

Analysis paralysis isn't just about having too much data. It's about having data without agreement on what the data means and your next actions.

"We have a data-driven culture," he told me.

I paused. "You have a data-defended culture," I said. "And there's a critical difference. In a data-driven culture, information opens conversations. In a data-defended culture, information ends them. Your people have learned that the right numbers matter more than the right conversations. So they give you numbers. And the conversations that actually matter have stopped happening in the room where you could do something about them."

He got defensive first. He started to respond the way leaders respond when they hear something that is true but unwelcome. He referenced the dashboards. The rigor of the monthly reviews. The fact that his team had more information available to them than any team he had previously led. I let him finish.

Then something shifted subtly, the way it shifts when a person stops arguing with what they just heard and starts sitting with it instead. He looked at me and said, "Say that again." I did. He looked down at the table. He picked up his pen and wrote something on the legal pad in front of him. I did not ask what it was. I did not need to. The fact that he wrote it down told me what I needed to know. The conversation had moved from something he was receiving to something he was beginning to own.

The fix wasn't more data. It was less, but with more honesty around what it meant.

We built a Trust Signal Dashboard™ Four measures. Not forty. Four. One page. Reviewed monthly. Not because four was a magic number, but because four was few enough that nobody could hide behind complexity and everyone had to stand next to what the numbers actually said.

One engagement indicator, something that told the truth about whether people were genuinely participating or just present. One execution indicator, something that measured whether work was getting done or getting reworked. One quality indicator, something that reflected whether outputs were meeting the standard or just meeting the deadline. And one capacity indicator, something that showed whether the organization was sustainable or burning down reserves.

Four numbers. On one page. Reviewed monthly.

Then we established the rule that changed everything: data is used to learn, not to blame. Before anyone could ask "Who caused this?" they had to first ask "What does this suggest?" That sequence matters because when blame comes first, people hide the data that makes them vulnerable. When learning comes first, people surface the data that makes the organization smarter.

The first meeting under the new discipline was uncomfortable. Leaders who had spent months weaponizing metrics suddenly had to sit with information without spinning it. They had to ask genuine questions instead of rhetorical ones. They had to admit what they didn't know.

Within 60 days, the shift was real.

Engagement improved because meetings became safer. People could share unfavorable data without fear of being targeted. The parking lot conversations moved back into the room. Candor increased. And when candor increases, the quality of decisions follows, because the decisions are being made based on reality instead of on curated presentations.

Performance improved because the team finally agreed on what mattered most and acted on it, with alignment and focus. When you reduce forty metrics to four, you force alignment. People stop arguing about which numbers matter because the decision has already been made. The energy shifts from debate to action.

"I thought data would be the answer. I was wrong. My team wasn't waiting for better data. They were waiting for me to lead with enough clarity that the data could do its job."

Data doesn't create clarity.
Leadership creates clarity.

Clarity removes the ambiguity that allows doubt to grow. But clarity alone is not enough. Leaders must also act on what is now clear, even when action is uncomfortable. That is the final pillar and the one that holds all the others accountable: Courage.

CHAPTER 9: COURAGE—TIMELY ACTION DESPITE DISCOMFORT

Courage is not fearlessness. It's acting despite discomfort.

The leader who delays a hard conversation isn't less courageous because they feel anxiety. They're less courageous because they let anxiety determine their timeline.

"The conversation you keep avoiding is the one your team is already having without you." —Gearl Loden

Courage is demonstrated through timing, not emotion.

The Timing Problem

Most leaders don't avoid hard decisions forever. They delay them. They know a performance conversation needs to happen, but they wait for "the right time." They know a failing project should be stopped, but they give it "one more quarter." They know a standard is eroding, but they hope it will self-correct.

The delay feels reasonable. It feels prudent. It feels like patience. But delay is costly. Every day a performance issue goes unaddressed, high performers lose trust. Every week a failing project continues, resources are wasted. Every month a standard slides, it becomes harder to reset.

Delayed courage is abdication.

What Courage Actually Means

Courage is not being comfortable with conflict, never feeling fear or anxiety, or acting impulsively without thinking.

Courage is addressing issues within 72 hours rather than 72 days, naming problems when they're small rather than waiting until they're crises, and holding standards when enforcement is uncomfortable.

Test: How long does it take you to address an issue after you notice it? If the answer is "weeks" or "months," look closely at courage as your fracture point.

The Three Forms of Courage

Form 1: Conversational Courage

The willingness to have hard conversations quickly.

Leaders without conversational courage delay feedback until annual reviews, avoid naming underperformance, hope problems resolve themselves, and communicate concerns indirectly through phrases like "some people have mentioned."

Leaders with conversational courage address issues within 72 hours, name problems directly, and create clear timelines for improvement. They say things like, "Your attendance has been below standard for the past two months." "I've noticed you're disengaged in team meetings." "Here's what needs to change, and here's the timeline we're working within."

Form 2: Decisional Courage

The willingness to make calls when outcomes are uncertain.

Leaders without decisional courage gather endless data to delay deciding, wait for consensus before acting, reverse decisions at the first sign of resistance, and blame circumstances when things go wrong.

Leaders with decisional courage decide with 80% of information rather than demanding 100%, move forward without full consensus, hold decisions even when challenged, and own outcomes, whether good or bad.

Form 3: Standards Courage

The willingness to enforce standards when enforcement is costly.

Leaders without standards courage make exceptions to avoid conflict, lower bars when people struggle, tolerate poor performance from high-status individuals, and let standards erode quietly.

Leaders with standards courage hold standards even when it's unpopular, apply rules evenly with no favoritism, address violations immediately, and accept that enforcement may cost relationships.

How Courage Breaks

Courage breaks in three predictable ways:

Erosion Pattern 1: Waiting for "The Right Time"

Leaders delay hard conversations, waiting for the right moment, the right words, the right emotional state, and the right conditions. But the "right time" seldom comes. Meanwhile, the issue compounds.

The Fix: The right time is now, or within 72 hours of noticing the issue. If you're waiting for perfect conditions, you're avoiding, not preparing.

Erosion Pattern 2: Softening Feedback Until It's Meaningless

Leaders deliver feedback but wrap it in so much context that the message gets lost.

Weak courage (softened beyond usefulness): *"I wanted to check in because I know you've been working really hard and I appreciate your effort, and I also know this has been a challenging quarter for everyone, so I just wanted to mention that* *there might be some opportunities for us to think about how we approach deadlines, but no pressure, just something to keep in mind."*

Strong courage (clear and direct): *"You've missed two deadlines this month. That's affecting the team. What's happening?"*

The weak version feels kinder. It's not. It's confusing.

The Fix: Lead with the problem. Then add context if needed.

Erosion Pattern 3: Avoiding Until Forced

Leaders know something needs addressing, but they wait until someone else complains, the problem becomes a crisis, or they're forced by policy or HR. By then, trust is already broken.

The Fix: Act when you first notice the issue, not when you're forced to act.

The 72-Hour Rule

When you notice an issue that requires action, you have 72 hours to address it. Not 72 days. Not "when the time is right." Seventy-two hours.

Why 72 hours? Because it's enough time to prepare, short enough to prevent drift, and it prevents overthinking from becoming avoidance.

The application is direct. Day one: you notice a pattern. Missed deadlines, declining quality, and an attitude shift. Day two: You prepare, gather specific examples, and plan the conversation. Day three: You have the conversation.

After 72 hours, delay becomes avoidance.

Courage in Practice: Intense Moments of Fellowship

There is a particular kind of courage that leadership demands when you already know what needs to be done, and you also know that doing it will unsettle people. Not because the decision is wrong. Because growth is uncomfortable, and necessary change almost always disturbs someone's equilibrium before it delivers its results.

Leading an organization means navigating alignment on multiple fronts simultaneously. It is not enough to bring your team along. You must also bring your board, because more than any other constituency, they determine whether your leadership has traction or friction. A board that is aligned does not eliminate hard moments, but a board that is not aligned turns every hard moment into a test of survival.

Major hires, staffing additions, staffing reductions, and significant policy changes all require courage, not because leaders do not know what to do, but because the path forward includes resistance that is predictable. A former board member I worked with put it better than I could. When a contentious decision was on the table, he would look around the room and say, *"Well, this is going to be one of those intense moments of fellowship."* He meant it with warmth and wisdom. He understood that the hardest decisions are the ones that test, and ultimately strengthen a leadership team if the leader has done the work to earn the room's trust before the moment arrives.

I faced this directly while leading through a recession. Budgets were shrinking, and the decisions were real: reducing positions through attrition, moving staff to new roles and buildings, and eliminating a small number of positions that my leadership team had identified as the right reductions to make. Some of those positions had direct, personal connections to board members and community leaders. The creative tension in those conversations was not subtle, but neither was the preparation behind our recommendations.

We had done the homework. We built the case with data, with equity in mind, and with a clear, honest articulation of the why. When we brought those recommendations forward, not defensively, but transparently, the dialogue shifted. The tension did not disappear, but it became productive. Board members with personal stakes in the outcome asked hard questions, and we answered them honestly. In the end, the recommendations were not just approved. They were supported.

That is the difference between courage and recklessness. Recklessness moves without preparation. Courage moves through the discomfort because the work is already done.

Do your homework. Make informed decisions. Surround yourself with people who will tell you the truth, not just what you want to hear. Then have the Courage to move forward. Your employees, your team, and your organization need that courage to set the stage for what comes next.

The room will not always be comfortable. That is not a sign you are wrong. It is a sign you are leading.

The Courage Diagnostic

Conversational Courage: What conversation have you been avoiding? How long has it been since you noticed the issue? What's the cost of waiting another 30 days?

Decisional Courage: What decision are you delaying because you don't have perfect information? Are you gathering data, or are you avoiding deciding? If you had to decide today with what you know now, what would you choose?

Standards Courage: What standard has been eroding? Have you made exceptions you shouldn't have? Who are you protecting by not enforcing the standard?

If you can identify issues in any category that have been unaddressed for 30+ days, courage is your fracture point.

Courage vs. Cruelty

Some leaders confuse courage with bluntness. They deliver feedback harshly and call it "being direct." But cruelty isn't courage.

Courage is direct and respectful, clear and compassionate, firm and fair. Cruelty is blunt without showing empathy, disguising punishment as feedback, and humiliating others publicly.

You can be courageous without being cruel. In fact, the most courageous conversations are often the most compassionate, because they're honest about the problem and supportive in addressing it.

The Toyota Principle: Stop the Line

Toyota has a fundamental rule: any worker can stop the entire production line if they spot a quality problem. Not because stopping the line is easy. Because fixing a defect early is always cheaper than fixing it late.

A defect caught on the line takes minutes. A defect caught after the car is built takes hours. A defect caught after the car is sold destroys trust.

The same principle applies to leadership. Address the issue early, and it's a conversation. Wait, and it becomes a formal process. Wait longer and it becomes a termination. The issue didn't get worse overnight. You just let time upgrade the response.

Courage isn't waiting for the perfect moment. It's stopping the line when you see the defect.

And of all seven pillars, Courage is the most time-sensitive. The longer you wait, the more expensive the fix. The two moments that follow test whether you can act within the window that matters.

Trust in Action: Two Moments That Test Courage

Moment: The Performance Issue Everyone Sees, But You Haven't Addressed

Context: You're a manager. One of your veteran employees has stopped engaging and is missing deadlines, skipping meetings, and delivering minimal effort. Other employees are covering for him. You've noticed but haven't acted because "he's had a tough year" and "he's close to retirement."

The Trust Test: Do you continue giving him grace, hoping it resolves itself? Have a direct conversation now, even if uncomfortable? Or document quietly and wait for a major incident?

Pillars Tested: Courage, Care, Consistency

What Strong Leaders Do: They address it directly with support and clarity.

"I need to talk about something I should have addressed sooner. Over the past three months, I've seen you (give specific examples): missing team meetings, turning in incomplete or late assignments, and showing a lack of engagement. I know this year has been hard, and I care about your well-being. But right now, this gap is affecting the team and our productivity. Here's what needs to change. Here's the support I'll provide. And here's the timeline: I need to see improvement within 30 days. Can we talk about what you need to make that happen?"

Why This Works: It names specific behaviors rather than vague concerns, balances care with standards because both matter, provides support that demonstrates investment, and states a timeline that creates urgency.

The Trust Leak: Every day the issue goes unaddressed, high performers lose trust. They conclude that standards are negotiable and effort is optional. Avoiding hard conversations is not kindness; it's abdication.

Moment: The Sales Platform Rollout That Needs to Die (But Everyone's Invested)

Context: You're a chief revenue officer. Eighteen months ago, you rolled out a new CRM + sales enablement stack companywide. You trained the entire sales organization. You reworked processes. Marketing built campaigns around the new workflow. The CEO referenced it in a town hall. But it's not working. Forecast accuracy hasn't improved. Cycle time is longer. Reps complain the system adds friction. Adoption is inconsistent, and managers are running "shadow spreadsheets" to get deals across the line.

The Trust Test: Do you keep tweaking fields and workflows, hoping it stabilizes? Pull the plug and own the failure? Or let it quietly decay while everyone pretends it's "still rolling out"?

Pillars Tested: Courage, Clarity, Character

What Strong Leaders Do: They stop it, name why, and extract the learning publicly.

At the leadership team meeting

"We need to address the CRM rollout. We launched it 18 months ago, expecting better forecasting, cleaner handoffs, and faster execution. We're not getting that. Forecast accuracy hasn't improved, cycle time is up, and adoption is inconsistent. The tool isn't the problem; the design is. We scaled a workflow that didn't fit our selling reality. That's on me. I should have piloted this with two regions and two deal motions before going companywide. I didn't, and I won't repeat that mistake.

We're discontinuing this workflow at quarter-end. Here's what we're keeping. Here's what we're stopping. Here's what we learned. I'm not asking anyone to pretend this was fine. I'm asking you to help me turn it into a better operating decision next time."

At the executive/board update

"I'm recommending we sunset the current CRM workflow at the end of the quarter. Based on adoption, performance metrics, and field feedback, it's not producing the outcomes we committed to. This is a leadership call. We chose a system design that didn't fit our selling motions, and we scaled before we proved it. Here's what we learned and how we'll run future rollouts: pilot, proof, then scale."

Why This Works

It stops drift (courage). It tells the truth without spin (clarity). It owns the decision publicly (character). And it converts failure into institutional learning (competence).

The Trust Leak

Leaders who let failing rollouts linger teach three things: reality is negotiable, appearances beat outcomes, and new initiatives aren't meant to work, just to be announced. Every additional month of "forced adoption" quietly drains credibility.

The Courage Diagnostic

Ask yourself: How long have I known it wasn't working? What am I protecting: my judgment, the vendor decision, or the CEO's public endorsement? What's the cost of forcing this for another quarter? If I were advising another CRO, what would I tell them?

Common Rationalizations Leaders Use

Rationalization 1: "We just need more time."
Reality: Time doesn't fix a misfit system design.

Rationalization 2: "We've invested too much."
Reality: Sunk cost doesn't justify future drag.

Rationalization 3: "It'll look bad to stop."
Reality: It looks worse to pretend.

Rationalization 4: "People will lose confidence."
Reality: They lose confidence when leaders dodge reality.

Follow-Up Action (3-week cadence)

Week 1: Debrief with sales and ops: what failed, what signals we ignored, and what we'd pilot differently.
Week 2: Communicate the learning to the organization in plain language, no blame, clear next steps.
Week 3: Apply the learning to the replacement: pilot with tight success metrics before any scale-up.

The Trust Paradox

Handled well, stopping a failing initiative increases trust more than a successful initiative ever could. Why? Because teams don't trust leaders who never fail. They trust leaders who fail, learn, and adjust quickly.

Stopping what isn't working signals that you're watching the data, that you care more about results than ego, that you won't waste their time on things that don't matter, and that you'll be honest when things go wrong. That's the foundation of trust.

Your System Check:

- *What will you address in the next 72 hours?*

These scenarios test your willingness to act, but courage isn't a single moment; it's a practice. The following stories show what happens when leaders find that practice and what it costs when they don't.

LEADERSHIP IN PRACTICE: COURAGE

Personal Story—The Conversation I Almost Didn't Have

I sat with it longer than I should have.

Not because I didn't know what to say. I did. I just didn't want the moment that comes after you say it, the moment when the air changes, and you can't go back to the version of the relationship where everything is fine. You can't laugh your way out. You can't pretend you didn't notice. Once it's spoken, it becomes real.

This was a relationship with history. Shared wins. Mutual respect. Showing up when it counted. We had built trust through consistency. We hadn't tested it through tension.

So I did what a lot of leaders do when the stakes feel personal. I delayed. I told myself it wasn't urgent. I told myself it would work itself out. I told myself I didn't want to make it awkward.

But the truth was simpler. Avoiding the conversation wasn't keeping the peace. It was creating a vacuum, and vacuums don't stay empty. They are filled with assumptions.

A tone gets misread. A delayed response starts to feel intentional. A short answer becomes a signal. You start assigning motives to things you never verified. Frustration grows quietly. And because nothing is said, the other person doesn't get a chance to correct what you're assuming.

That's how trust starts leaking. Not through betrayal. Through silence.

I could feel it happening in me. I was becoming less curious and more certain. I was building a case in my own head by collecting small moments as evidence; and once you start building a case, you stop building understanding.

The most dangerous part is what it does to your posture. You stop asking direct questions. You start withholding information, not as punishment, but as protection. You keep your tone neutral while your assumptions get louder. You don't say, "I'm feeling distant." You say, "All good."

And then you wonder why it keeps getting worse.

I remember the familiar tightening in my chest, the moment right before emotional risk. The moment when you can still choose comfort instead.

I almost did.

What stopped me wasn't bravery. It was clarity. I realized that if I didn't speak, the story in my head would become the story between us; and once that happens, even good people start treating each other like threats.

So I had the conversation. Not perfectly. Not with a confident voice. No dramatic opening line. Just honest. I said what had been sitting with me. I named what I was noticing. I owned what I didn't know. And I admitted the part that felt most vulnerable: that I didn't want to assume bad intentions, but I was starting to. I didn't want to withdraw, but I could feel myself doing it.

Then there was a pause. The kind where you start rewriting your words in real time and preparing to regret them.

And then something happened that seldom happens when you avoid the conversation: the other person didn't get defensive. They were present. They shared what I didn't see. They clarified what I had misread. They named something I hadn't considered. In that moment, the relationship stopped being a guessing game. It became a conversation again.

Everything didn't resolve neatly. Not every feeling disappeared. Not every detail landed perfectly. But something shifted. The goodwill returned to the room.

That matters more than people realize.

Because trust isn't built by avoiding hard conversations. Trust is built when you're willing to sit in discomfort long enough to stay honest. When you're willing to risk awkwardness to preserve a connection. When you choose clarity over quiet resentment.

That conversation didn't fix everything. It did something even more foundational. It reopened the door. It signaled good intent. It interrupted the drift.

And it reminded me of what I've had to learn more than once: when important conversations don't happen, frustration doesn't stay contained. It leaks into tone. It leaks into assumptions. It leaks into withheld information. It leaks into how people interpret each other's actions, and it erodes trust.

But when you dare to have the conversation, imperfectly, humanly, you give trust a fighting chance. Not because the outcome is guaranteed. Because goodwill is visible again.

And once goodwill is visible, trust can be rebuilt.

Story 9.1—The Conversation Everyone Delayed

Everyone saw it. That was the part that made it worse.

The issue had been visible for months. A pattern of behavior that was corroding the team's trust, dragging down performance, and creating a two-tier culture where one person operated under different rules than everyone else. People talked about it privately. Managers referenced it guardedly in one-on-ones. The leader acknowledged it in the most indirect terms: "We have some dynamics we need to work through."

But no one named it. Not directly. Not clearly. Not to the person whose behavior was causing the damage.

The longer it lingered, the more expensive it became. Not just in performance, though that was real, but in credibility. Every day the issue went unaddressed, here's what the organization concluded about leadership: they see it, and they won't act on it. That conclusion didn't stay contained. It leaked into every other interaction. If leadership won't hold the standard here, can they be trusted to hold it anywhere?

That's the hidden cost of delayed courage. It doesn't just affect the situation you're avoiding. It affects the organization's belief in whether standards mean anything at all.

The leader knew. When we sat down, she didn't need me to diagnose the problem. She needed me to help her stop avoiding it.

"I keep telling myself I need more information," she said. "But I think I have enough. I think I've had enough for a while."

That's one of the most honest things a leader can say. Because the gap between knowing something needs to be addressed and actually addressing it is where leadership credibility is often lost. Not in the difficult conversation itself, but in the months of silence that preceded it.

We used the 72-Hour Rule because the discipline of acting within a defined window broke the cycle of infinite delay. She committed: within 72 hours, she would have the conversation. Privately. Directly. Respectfully.

We built the conversation around five clear statements. "Here's what's happening" is observable behavior, not character assessment. "Here's the standard." What leadership in this organization looks like, stated plainly, without apology. "Here's why this matters," not just for performance, but for trust; she named the impact on the team, on the culture, and on the organization's ability to operate with confidence. "Here's what changes now," a clear expectation with a clear timeline and a clear definition of what "better" looks like. And "Here's how we'll measure it," not vague promises to "do better," but a specific follow-up in two weeks, with observable benchmarks.

She opened the conversation with the hardest sentence most leaders avoid: "I should have had this conversation sooner. The fact that I didn't is on me, but I'm having it now because the standard matters more than my comfort."

That opening did two things. It owned the delay without making excuses. And it framed the conversation not as punishment, but as a commitment to the culture.

The conversation lasted less than twenty minutes. It wasn't dramatic. It wasn't emotional. It was clear. And clarity, in these moments, is its own form of respect.

The conversation alone wasn't enough. Courage in these situations requires follow-through. So she reinforced the standard with consistent action over the next two months. She held the follow-up meeting. She measured the behavior against the benchmarks. She acknowledged improvement where it appeared and named the continued gaps where they persisted.

The impact wasn't limited to the person who received the feedback. The entire organization felt it. Engagement increased because people saw that leadership was willing to protect the culture. In organizations where issues linger, people learn a devastating lesson: the standard is aspirational, not operational. When leadership acts, that lesson reverses. People start believing that the values are real, that the expectations apply to everyone, and that their own commitment to the standard is matched at the top.

Performance improved because teams stopped wasting energy on avoidance and workaround strategies. When the dysfunction is named and addressed, the informal systems people built to compensate become unnecessary. Energy flows back to the work.

Courage is the most time-sensitive of all leadership disciplines. The longer you wait, the more it costs, not just you, but also everyone who's been watching and waiting for you to act.

Story 9.2—The Meeting I Almost Cancelled

Earlier in my career, I noticed something that worried me.

It wasn't a crisis. It wasn't a scandal. It was a drift, a slow shift in how decisions were being made above me that I believed was going to cost the organization. I could see a pattern forming that the people around me either didn't see or didn't want to name, and the person who needed to hear it was my boss.

Let me be transparent about what that felt like. It felt like standing at the edge of a cliff and choosing to step forward anyway.

My boss was someone I respected. Deeply capable. Committed to the mission. The kind of leader who has earned their authority through years of results. Questioning their direction wasn't just professionally risky; it felt personally uncomfortable. Because I wasn't trying to challenge them. I was trying to support them. I just wasn't sure they'd hear it that way.

I spent three days thinking about whether to say anything. I ran the scenarios in my head the way leaders do when the stakes feel personal. If I say this and they receive it well, trust deepens. If I say this and they don't receive it well, I've damaged a relationship I value and possibly put myself in a difficult position. If I say nothing and I'm right, I've watched something go wrong that I could have prevented. If I say nothing and I'm wrong, I have worried for nothing, but I've also practiced silence when I should have practiced honesty.

That last scenario is the one that moved me, because I realized that staying quiet wasn't neutral. Silence, when you see something that matters, is a choice that erodes your own integrity over time. Every time you see something and don't say it, you teach yourself that comfort is more important than truth. Do that enough times, and you become the kind of leader who only speaks when it's safe. That's not leading; that's performing.

So I asked for the meeting.

I didn't ambush. I didn't wait for a hallway moment or try to slip it into another conversation. I sent a direct request: "I'd like twenty minutes to share some observations and concerns. I want to be honest with you about something I'm seeing, and I'd rather do it face to face."

That message alone was a trust signal, whether my boss recognized it or not. It said, "I respect you enough to be direct." I trust this relationship enough to risk discomfort. I believe in what we're building enough to protect it, even when protecting it means saying something hard.

Walking into that meeting, I had no guarantee of how it would land. I'd prepared what I wanted to say. I'd grounded it in observable patterns, not assumptions. I'd framed it around the mission, not my own preferences. And I'd decided before I walked through the door: even if this doesn't go well, I'll know I did the right thing.

That decision, made before the outcome was known, is where courage lives. Not in the moment it works out, but in the moment you choose to act without knowing whether it will work.

I laid out what I was seeing. Plainly. Without softening it into uselessness, but without making it adversarial. I said something close to, "I'm noticing a pattern in how we're approaching these decisions, and I'm concerned that if it continues, we're going to face consequences that will be harder to fix later. I could be wrong, but I'd rather share what I'm seeing now than wish I had six months from now."

Then I stopped talking. That part was harder than initiating the conversation.

My boss was quiet for a moment, and in that silence, I felt every version of regret I'd been rehearsing. Maybe I'd overstepped. Maybe I'd misread the pattern. Maybe I should have stayed in my lane.

Then my boss said something I didn't expect: "I've been sensing some of this, too. I just didn't have anyone frame it the way you just did."

That sentence changed the trajectory of our relationship. My boss didn't agree with everything I said; they pushed back on some of it, and they were right to. But the conversation opened a channel that hadn't existed before. My boss now knew I was someone who would tell them the truth, even when the truth was uncomfortable. And I now knew my boss was someone who could receive hard feedback without punishing the person who brought it.

That's what courage builds when it's practiced well. Not agreement but trust. My boss didn't need me to be right about everything. They needed to know I wouldn't hide what I was seeing. I didn't need my boss to accept every concern. I needed to know the relationship could hold honesty without breaking.

In the months that followed, my boss came to me more often for candid input because I'd proven myself willing to be honest when it was hard. That willingness became a form of value that had nothing to do with my title or my expertise. It was trust, earned through a single act of courage that could have gone either way.

Here's what I've learned since then, after decades on both sides of that table: the leaders who earn the deepest trust aren't the ones who always have the right answer. They're the ones who are willing to walk into a room, say what needs to be said, and accept whatever comes next.

Courage isn't knowing the conversation will go well. Courage is having the conversation because it needs to happen, regardless of how it goes. And when it does go well, the trust it builds is stronger than anything you could have earned by staying silent.

Story 9.3—The Conversation That Cost Thirty Days

I want to tell you about the thirty days I spent not having a conversation I knew I needed to have.

A high performer on my team had developed a pattern I didn't like. Her work was exceptional. She continued to produce at a high level, but she started arriving late to leadership meetings. Not by an hour. By seven or eight minutes. Consistently. Without acknowledgement.

It sounds small. It wasn't.

She was a model for the newer leaders on the team. What she normalized in small moments, they would assume was permissible. Several other people noticed. I could see it in the way their eyes tracked when she walked in. No one said anything. No one had to.

I told myself I would address it when the moment was right. The moment was never right. We were deep in a major initiative. She was carrying more than her share. I rationalized that she'd earned the grace. The truth was simpler: I was conflict-averse about people I respected, and I let that avoidance become a pattern.

Thirty days in, a mid-level leader came to me. "I need to understand something," she said. "Is tardiness to leadership meetings optional? Because I've started seeing it more broadly, and I don't know if the standard has changed."

The standard hadn't changed. But my enforcement of it had. By staying silent, I had effectively changed it.

I had the conversation that afternoon. It was direct, professional, and brief. She hadn't registered the impact. She corrected it immediately and without defensiveness. She was, as I expected, a professional.

But the thirty days had cost something I couldn't recover. Not with her. With everyone who had watched me not act and drawn their own conclusions about what the standards were.

Here is what I know now: courage isn't only about the content of the conversation. It's about the timing of it. The longer you wait, the louder your silence becomes. Your team is always reading the gap between what you say you value and what you are willing to protect. That gap is where trust breaks.

The Seven Pillars—Quick Reference

Which pillar is at risk? Match the signal to the pattern.

Pillar	Core Discipline	Key Signal
Character	Values when they're expensive	Standards enforced selectively
Consistency	Predictable behavior under pressure	People say it "depends on the day."
Communication	Remove uncertainty before it spreads	People ask for updates you haven't given
Competence	Systems over heroics	Team can't execute without you
Care	Protection, not paternalism	High performers are burning out or leaving
Clarity	Truth faster than rumor	People guessing what you actually meant
Courage	Timely action despite discomfort	Delays measured in weeks, not hours

PART THREE—RUNNING THE SYSTEM

CHAPTER 10: THE LEADERSHIP LEDGER™

"Trust has a ledger. Leaders who read it weekly rarely face a deficit they can't recover from." — Gearl Loden

Trust is not all-or-nothing.

It doesn't exist in two states: present or absent.

Trust is a running record of how your decisions land.

Every action either strengthens the system or stresses it.

Leaders who understand this principle manage trust deliberately. They track what builds trust and what depletes it. They monitor the balance before it goes negative.

Leaders who don't understand this stress the system without realizing it until it fails under load.

How the Leadership Ledger™ Works

Think of the Ledger as a record of how your decisions land over time, not what you intended, but what people experienced.

Deposits are the actions that build character, clarity, competence, care, communication, consistency, or courage. These increase the trust balance. They don't need to be dramatic. Most deposits are small: a commitment kept, a decision explained, a standard applied evenly. What matters is that they accumulate.

Withdrawals are the actions that erode consistency, create confusion, demonstrate incompetence, ignore capacity, violate values, withhold information, or delay hard decisions. These decrease the trust balance. Like deposits, most withdrawals are small: a priority shift that wasn't communicated, an exception that wasn't explained, or a conversation that was avoided. Individually forgettable. Collectively devastating.

The record tells the story. When the system is operating well, people give you the benefit of the doubt. Execution is smooth. Recovery from mistakes is fast. When the system is under stress, trust becomes fragile. Mistakes are costly, execution is slow, and small issues trigger disproportionate reactions. When the system is broken, trust is gone. Repair becomes difficult. People assume the worst intentions behind every decision. Turnover increases, and the best people leave first.

Building trust is slow.

Each consistent behavior, each clear communication, and each courageous decision make a small deposit.

Over time, deposits compound.

But withdrawals happen fast.

One inconsistent response under pressure can erase weeks of deposits.

One withheld piece of information can erase months of transparency.

One delayed conversation can erase years of credibility.

THE TRUST-PROTECTION SEQUENCE™

Running the Second Track Before High-Stakes Decisions

The Leadership Ledger™ tells you where the system stands. The Trust-Protection Sequence™ is how you protect it before a high-stakes decision creates erosion you didn't plan for

In the Introduction, I shared the story of the season that broke my understanding of leadership, the decision I made too fast, the governance meeting that exposed the leak, and the hard realization that intent doesn't protect trust. Systems do.

What I built from that failure is what you're about to read.

I call it the Trust-Protection Sequence™. It's not a communication strategy. It's not a checklist you hand to your team. It's a leadership discipline, a set of moves I run internally before any decision that carries real consequences.

Every high-stakes decision creates two tracks of work. The first is the decision itself, strategy, data, and action. The second is the trust architecture around the decision, how it lands, what meaning people attach to the process, and whether the system stays steady or starts to fracture. Leaders who skip the second track don't just create isolated erosion. They risk a systemic breakdown.

Here are the seven moves.

Step 1: Slow Down Long Enough to Name the Real Risk

Before I move, I ask the questions that would've saved me earlier: How might this decision be misread? Will it feel like control instead of leadership? Will speed look like disregard? Will decisiveness be mistaken for dismissiveness? Will people see efficiency or exclusion?

Most leaders think the risk is the outcome. Often, the bigger risk is the meaning people attach to the process.

Once I name the risk, I separate the work into two tracks: the decision and the trust moves that keep the system steady. I do this alone first, then bring it to my team, not to rehearse answers but to pressure-test assumptions. What I miss in my own read, someone closer to the ground floor catches in theirs.

This step takes minutes. Skipping it can cost months.

Step 2: Run the Clarity Sequence—Before Anyone Can Guess

When leaders move quickly, ambiguity is the accelerant that turns concern into rumor. So I communicate in a specific order. Every time.

The headline: What's changing? The why: the constraint or reality driving it. What's not changing: the anchor people need. The timeline: what happens when. The decision rights: who decides what. The next touchpoint: when we'll update again.

That order matters. When you skip "what's not changing," people start protecting themselves. When you skip "decision rights," people as-sume politics. When you skip "next touchpoint," people start inventing their own updates.

Clarity isn't about saying more. It's about removing the need for speculation.

Step 3: Design Consistency Into the Process—So It Doesn't Feel Mood-Driven

People don't need you to be perfect. They need you to be predictable.

I codify the standard before the decision goes public: what inputs matter, what data we use, what voices are consulted, and what values guide trade-offs. When feasible, I build stakeholder voice into the decision itself, not after the direction is set, but while it's being shaped. Decisions built with stakeholder fingerprints on them land differently than decisions delivered to stakeholders after the fact.

Step 4: Make Care Visible — Protection, Not Paternalism

Care that lives only in a leader's heart doesn't reach the team. It has to show up in the structure.

I build protection into the rollout; I name what this will cost people in time, energy, and learning curve. I identify the pressure points. I add support structures before I add expectations. And I look to remove one burden as I introduce a new demand.

Care becomes credible when people can point to something concrete and say, "The leader thought about what this would do to us." That's the difference between a leader who cares and a system that protects. Both matter. Only the second survives when pressure increases.

Step 5: Create a Clean Channel for Dissent — Before It Goes Underground

If you don't create a safe place for disagreement, it won't disappear. It will relocate to hallways, group texts, and parking lot conversations that never make it back to where decisions are made.

So I invite dissent on purpose: "What am I missing? Where will this break? What feels unfair?" Then I respond without punishment. I don't shame the question. I don't label it as negativity. I treat it as intelligence.

When leaders can receive dissent, teams stop needing politics. When leaders punish it, even subtly, even with a tone shift, teams learn to perform agreement instead of offering truth.

Step 6: Prove the Standard With Action — Not Reassurance

This is the step that turns trust talk into trust.

After any high-stakes decision, I look for the earliest opportunity to demonstrate that the process I described is actually how I operate. The fastest way to reinforce trust is to show people something they can point to: "They did what they said."

Reassurance is cheap. Proof is not.

Step 7: Hold the Line When Pressure Tests It

The sequence isn't tested in calm conditions. It's tested the first time the decision gets challenged, the first time a shortcut looks attractive, and the first time holding the standard costs something.

Leaders who hold the standard under pressure, who communicate proactively when silence would be easier, who invite dissent when agreement would be faster, and who protect capacity when cutting it would be convenient, build a trust balance that compounds over time.

The leaders who struggle most with trust often aren't the ones who make bad decisions. They're the ones who make good decisions without protecting trust.

The Trust-Protection Sequence™ gives leaders the system to protect trust.

Common Deposits

What builds trust?

The behaviors are specific, and they map directly to the seven pillars.

Character deposits come from choosing values over convenience, admitting mistakes publicly rather than quietly correcting them, and applying standards to yourself with the same rigor you apply to others. Character deposits are expensive at the moment and invaluable over time.

Consistency deposits come from responding to similar situations similarly, explaining when and why you change approaches, and enforcing standards evenly across people and circumstances. When people can predict how you'll respond, they stop spending energy guessing and start spending it on the work.

Communication deposits come from explaining "why" before announcing "what," communicating proactively rather than reactively, and sharing partial information when full information isn't yet available. The instinct to wait until you have the complete picture is understandable, but silence doesn't feel like patience to the people waiting. It feels like being left out.

Competence deposits come from building systems that work without you, addressing capability gaps quickly rather than hoping they resolve, and piloting before scaling. Leaders who build competence and trust don't just deliver results; they build the infrastructure that makes results repeatable.

Care deposits come from removing work before adding more, protecting high-performer capacity instead of exploiting it, and enforcing boundaries around workload even when the pressure is real. Care isn't just about being nice. It's about demonstrating that the people doing the work matter as much as the work itself.

Clarity deposits come from naming uncomfortable truths directly, defining success in observable terms rather than aspirational ones, and distinguishing clearly between what's been decided and what's still open. Clarity is the pillar that prevents the most common source of organizational friction: people interpreting the same situation differently because no one named what was actually true.

Courage deposits come from addressing issues within 72 hours, having hard conversations early rather than waiting for the "right time," and stopping failing initiatives quickly instead of letting them consume resources while everyone privately knows they're not working.

Common Withdrawals

What erodes trust?

The same pillars that build trust destroy it when the behaviors reverse.

Character withdrawals happen when leaders choose convenience over stated values, apply standards selectively based on relationships or politics, or make exceptions for themselves that they wouldn't allow for anyone else. Character withdrawals are the most expensive because they erode the one thing that's hardest to rebuild: belief in the leader's integrity.

Consistency withdrawals happen when leaders respond differently to the same situation without explanation, make exceptions without naming them, or change standards silently. The damage isn't in the change itself; it's in the silence around it. When standards shift without acknowledgment, people stop trusting the standards.

Communication withdrawals happen when leaders withhold information to "protect" people, announce decisions without explaining the reasoning behind them, or soften the truth until it's meaningless. Every piece of information a leader holds back is a piece the team fills in with speculation, and speculation is almost always worse than reality.

Competence withdrawals happen when leaders promote people before they're ready, reward heroics instead of building systems, or repeat the same failures without adjusting. The team sees all of this. They may not say it directly, but they conclude whether the organization is capable of learning.

Care withdrawals happen when leaders add work without removing anything, overload high performers because they're reliable, or normalize unsustainable workloads as the cost of doing the job. The message, whether intended or not, is that output matters more than the people producing it.

Clarity withdrawals happen when leaders speak in vague generalities, leave interpretation to others rather than naming what's true, or avoid identifying problems directly. Ambiguity isn't neutral. It's a withdrawal that compounds quietly until the team stops trying to decode what the leader actually means.

Courage withdrawals happen when leaders delay hard conversations, wait for "the right time" that never arrives, or hope that problems will resolve themselves. Every day a necessary conversation is delayed is a day the team absorbs the cost of that avoidance.

Reading the System

Leaders often ask: "How much trust do I have?"

The answer: Read the system.

When the system is running well, the signals are unmistakable. You can make a decision, and people execute without questioning the reasoning. You can deliver critical feedback, and people receive it as helpful rather than threatening. You can make a mistake, and people assume good intent. You can change direction, and people adapt without cynicism. These aren't signs of a compliant team. They're signs of a team that trusts the leader enough to move forward without hedging.

When the system is under stress, the signals are equally clear. People start asking permission for things they used to own. Feedback is met with defensiveness. Mistakes trigger disproportionate reactions. Changes are met with resistance and speculation about hidden motives. These aren't signs of a difficult team. They're signs of a team that has learned to protect itself.

Rebuilding After Erosion

The good news: Trust can be rebuilt.

The bad news: Rebuilding takes longer than breaking.

If you erode trust significantly, break a promise, act inconsistently, or avoid a hard conversation, you can't restore it with a single visible act.

Consider this: You delay addressing a performance issue for three months. That's a visible erosion signal. Then you have the conversation. That's one repair action. But the team doesn't immediately trust that you'll address issues going forward. They need to see a pattern of timely action before the Ledger recovers.

Recovery: In practice, for every major withdrawal, leaders typically need multiple consistent deposits before the balance feels restored. There is no precise formula, but the gap is always wider than leaders expect.

This is why prevention is better than repair.

Tracking Your Ledger

Most leaders don't track deposits and withdrawals. They operate by feel.

That's risky.

Here's how to track deliberately.

Weekly Ledger Check (5 Minutes)

At the end of each week, run a brief audit structured around three questions. **First,** strengthening actions: what did you do this week that built trust, and which pillar did it strengthen? **Second,** erosion patterns: what did you do this week that eroded trust, and which pillar did it weaken? **Third,** System status: Is the system stronger or under more stress than last week, and what do you need to address in the week ahead?

The discipline isn't in the answers. It's in the habit of asking. Most leaders who start this practice are surprised by what surfaces. The withdrawals aren't dramatic. They're invisible until someone deliberately looks.

One caution: self-assessment has limits. The most valuable Ledger reviews happen when a trusted colleague, a direct report with psychological safety, or an executive coach can pressure-test what you're seeing. If your withdrawals list is consistently shorter than your deposits list, that's not necessarily a sign of a strong week. It may be a sign that you need someone else in the room.

Monthly Team Pulse

Once per month, step back from self-assessment and read the system signals. Are people bringing you issues early or waiting until the problems are too large to ignore? Are questions increasing or decreasing in meetings? Is execution smooth or heavy with friction? Are high performers engaged and volunteering or withdrawing and protecting their energy?

These signals reveal the balance better than any self-assessment. The team always knows the truth before the leader does.

The Ledger in Practice

Let's walk through a real scenario.

On Monday, a leader announces a budget cut without explaining why. That's a communication withdrawal and a clarity withdrawal. On Tuesday, the same leader delays addressing a performance issue they've been avoiding for weeks, a courage withdrawal. On Wednesday, they work late and send emails at eleven o'clock at night, implicitly signaling that responses are expected. That is a form of care withdrawal. On Thursday, they make an exception to a deadline for a favored employee without explanation, a consistency withdrawal, and a character withdrawal. On Friday, they have a one-on-one, listen well, and provide clear feedback, a communication deposit, and a clarity deposit.

Net for the week: Six trust-eroding actions, two trust-strengthening ones. System status: declining.

If this pattern continues for a month, trust will fracture. The Friday strengthening action doesn't compensate for the Monday-through-Thursday erosion. Trust is asymmetric in how it builds and how it breaks. It always has been.

The Compounding Effect

Trust compounds in both directions.

"Trust accumulates in patterns. It fractures in them too."

In high-trust environments, compounding works for you. People assume good intent when leaders make mistakes. Execution is fast because there's less overhead, fewer unnecessary approvals, and less political maneuvering. Innovation increases because psychological safety enables risk. Retention improves because people stay for the culture, not just the role. Every deposit makes the next deposit easier, and the returns accelerate.

In low-trust environments, compounding works against you. People assume bad intent when leaders make mistakes. Execution slows under the weight of documentation, cover-your-back behavior, and internal politics. Innovation stops because fear of failure dominates every calculation. Turnover increases, and the best people leave first because they have the most options. Every withdrawal makes the next withdrawal more damaging, and the erosion accelerates.

The difference between these environments isn't one decision.

It's the accumulated record of thousands of small decisions and their impact on the people who experienced them.

Your System Check:

- *Think about this past week.*
- *Did your actions strengthen or stress the system this week?*
- *If you stressed the system more than you strengthened it, which pillar needs attention this week?*

LEADERSHIP IN PRACTICE: THE LEADERSHIP LEDGER™

Most trust failures don't announce themselves. They show up as "Why is everything so heavy?"

The Leadership Ledger™ is how you stop paying that tax.

Story 10.1—The Invisible Tax

The team looked fine on the surface.

Their meetings were calm. Deliverables were moving. Nobody was openly upset or visibly disengaged. If you'd walked through the building on any given day, you would have seen a functioning organization doing respectable work.

The leader had inherited this team, and for the first few months, he had operated on the assumption that "fine" was fine. No fires meant no problems. The machine was running.

Why question it?

But something nagged at him. Something he couldn't put a name to.

"Everything takes more effort than it should," he told me during our first conversation. "I can't point to one thing that's broken. It just feels... heavy."

I've learned to pay close attention to that word. When a capable leader describes their organization as heavy, they're seldom talking about workload. They're describing friction. The invisible kind. The kind that lives between people, between expectations and reality, between what's being said in meetings and what's being said after them.

My questions didn't deal with strategy or performance metrics. Instead, I asked about behavior. About what decisions felt easy and which ones required extra meetings. About where people were agreeable in the room and cautious afterward. About whether the team debated openly or whether disagreements surfaced through indirection, through tone, through timing, or through strategic silence.

The pattern emerged quickly. The organization wasn't in crisis yet. But it was in debt. Trust debt.

The leader wasn't breaking trust through big mistakes or visible failures. He was breaking it through micro-inconsistencies, small shifts in priorities that weren't named. Quiet exceptions that weren't explained. Delayed follow-through that wasn't acknowledged. Each one, on its own, was minor, even forgettable. The kind of thing you'd never cite in a performance review or an exit interview. But together, accumulated over weeks and months, they created a tax that everyone in the system was paying without being able to name the charge.

"I don't think you have a communication problem," I told him. "I think you have several things occurring that are causing trust to leak. And it's small enough that you can't see it and steady enough that it's draining your capacity every week."

We introduced a Leadership Ledger™ rhythm as a discipline rather than as a form or spreadsheet. He committed to a fifteen-minute review every Friday, structured around three questions: Where did trust strengthen this week? Where did it leak, intentionally or not? And what is the one action I will take in the next seven days to strengthen the pillar most at risk?

The rule was to be detailed and specific. No vibes. No general feelings. Deposits had to be tied to observable actions: a clear decision communicated promptly; a standard applied consistently; a hard conversation handled with dignity; a commitment kept on time and without excuse. Withdrawals had to be tied to behaviors, too: a delayed decision that left people guessing; an exception made quietly that should have been named; silence during a moment of uncertainty; and accountability applied unevenly.

The first Friday review was eye-opening. He could name three deposits without much difficulty. But when he started listing withdrawals, the list grew longer than expected. Two priority shifts that hadn't been communicated. One commitment that had been quietly dropped. A standard that had been applied to one team member and not another. None of these were crises. All of them were leaks.

By the end of the month, the pattern was unmistakable. He wasn't creating distrust through any single action. He was creating it through accumulation, a steady drip of small inconsistencies that the team absorbed without comment because no single one was big enough to challenge; but the total was significant. The team was expending energy every day managing the uncertainty those inconsistencies created. Energy that should have been spent on the work.

We chose one standard to protect for thirty days: no silent exceptions. If something changed, it had to be named. If a priority shifted, the trade-off had to be explained. If a commitment couldn't be kept, he had to say so early, not after the damage. Not with an excuse. Just plainly: "This changed. Here's why. Here's what it means for you."

That single discipline changed the temperature of the organization within weeks.

By week four, he added a second protected standard: decision rights clarity. Who decides what? Who needs to be consulted? Who executes? The ambiguity around decision-making had been one of the largest sources of hidden friction, because people didn't know whether to act, wait, or escalate, so they defaulted to the safest option, which was doing nothing until the leader weighed in.

Within eight weeks, the results were tangible. Engagement rose because people stopped guessing. Performance improved because work stopped getting reworked. When direction is clear and consistent, teams naturally move forward. He reported fewer "alignment meetings" and more actual execution. Over time, the team became more open and honest with each other. They were more candid in meetings. More willing to name what wasn't working.

Honesty is one of the first signs that the system is stabilizing.

Near the end of our work together, he shared something that stopped me in my tracks and has stayed with me since.

"I always thought trust was about the big moments. Now I see it's about a hundred small ones I wasn't paying attention to."

CHAPTER 11: READING THE SIGNALS

"The signal you read today is the crisis you prevent tomorrow." — Gearl Loden

Trust doesn't break loudly.

It breaks quietly, through small behavioral shifts that most leaders miss. By the time trust issues are obvious, the damage is serious.

The leaders who maintain trust are the ones who read signals early and act before fractures become failures.

This chapter teaches you how to read the signals.

The Signal Detection Problem

Why do leaders miss trust drift? Three reasons shape the blind spot, and understanding each one is the first step toward seeing clearly.

Reason 1: Trust Information Flows with a Lag

Teams see trust fractures immediately. Leaders see them late. People don't say, "I don't trust you anymore." They show it through behavior: asking permission for things they used to decide, documenting conversations to protect themselves, reducing communication to the minimum required, and disengaging from optional contributions. These behaviors are visible, but only if leaders are watching for them.

Reason 2: Leaders Confuse Activity with Trust

Leaders see meetings happening, tasks getting completed, and people showing up and convince that everything is fine. But trust isn't measured by activity. It's measured by the quality of engagement. The real signal is in the texture of participation: Are people bringing issues early or waiting until forced? Are they asking questions to understand or to protect themselves? Are they volunteering solutions or waiting to be told? Activity can mask trust erosion for months.

Reason 3: Leaders Operate Inside Their Own Intent

Leaders experience their reasoning. Teams experience outcomes. When a leader makes a decision, they know why it was made, what constraints shaped it, and what trade-offs were considered. The team doesn't see any of that. They only see the outcome. So the leader thinks the decision makes perfect sense. The team thinks it's confusing and inconsistent. The leader misses the signal because they're inside their own perspective.

By the time the signal is loud enough to act on, it's been visible long enough to matter.

The Eight Trust Drift Signals

We introduced these signals in Chapter 2. Now we'll explain how to diagnose what each signal means and what to do about it. Leaders who learn to read these signals catch trust fractures early, when repair is still simple.

Signal 1: People Ask Permission for Things They Used to Decide Independently

What it means: Decision-making confidence has broken. See Chapter 2 for full signal analysis.

Pillar fracturing: *Consistency or Clarity*

Ask yourself whether you've changed expectations recently without explaining why, whether your responses to similar situations are predictable, and whether people know what success looks like. If the decision framework has shifted without explanation, people will retreat to permission-seeking as a form of self-protection.

Signal 2: Questions Decrease in Meetings

What it means: Asking questions has become unsafe or pointless. See Chapter 2 for full signal analysis.

Pillar fracturing: *Communication, Clarity, or Courage. When questions stop, it often signals that the leader's responses to dissent have made honesty feel costly.*

Ask yourself whether you've dismissed questions recently, whether you get defensive when challenged, and whether you're explaining the "why" behind decisions. Silence in a room that used to ask questions is not agreement; it's withdrawal.

Signal 3: Execution Slows—Even on Straightforward Tasks

What it means: People are protecting themselves rather than executing. See Chapter 2 for full signal analysis.

Pillar fracturing: *Care, Competence, or Consistency*

Ask yourself whether people trust the system or are protecting themselves, whether outcomes are predictable, and whether you've been micromanaging or second-guessing work you used to trust. Slowdowns aren't always a workload problem. They're often a safety problem.

Signal 4: High Performers Stop Volunteering for New Projects

What it means: High performers have stopped investing discretionary effort. See Chapter 2 for full signal analysis.

Pillar fracturing: *Care, Character, or Consistency*

Ask yourself whether you're rewarding high performance with more work, whether your best people are sustainable or breaking, and whether you've removed work before adding more. When high performers go quiet, something has shifted in their calculation about return on effort.

Signal 5: Rumors Spread Faster Than Official Communication

What it means: The rumor mill is moving faster than your messaging. See Chapter 2 for full signal analysis.

Pillar fracturing: *Communication, Clarity, or Courage*

Ask yourself whether you're withholding information, whether your communication is too slow or too vague, and whether you're waiting for "the right time" that never comes. When the rumor mill moves faster than your messaging, you've created a vacuum, and people fill vacuums with worst-case assumptions.

Signal 6: People Stop Bringing You Problems Early

What it means: Problems surface late because raising them early feels unsafe. See Chapter 2 for full signal analysis.

Pillar fracturing: *Consistency, Clarity, or Courage*

Ask yourself whether you've shot messengers, whether you delay addressing issues people bring you, and whether people feel safe bringing bad news. Problems that surface late aren't late; they're problems that were known early and not reported.

Signal 7: Conversations Happen "Around" You Instead of "with" You

What it means: Direct communication with you is no longer seen as productive. See Chapter 2 for full signal analysis.

Pillar fracturing: *Character, Communication, or Courage*

Ask yourself whether you've made it unsafe to bring hard truths, whether you get defensive when challenged, and whether you've punished honesty in the past. Bypass behavior is a symptom. The cause is almost always perceived risk.

Signal 8: Small Mistakes Trigger Disproportionate Emotional Reactions

What it means: Trust reserves are depleted, a late-stage signal requiring full system diagnosis. See Chapter 2 for full signal analysis.

Pillar fracturing: *Multiple pillars (this is a late-stage symptom)*

Ask yourself which pillar broke first, where the erosion started, and what pattern has been repeating. Disproportionate reactions are rarely about the immediate mistake. They're about accumulated distrust that finally has a safe outlet. Trace back to the original fracture.

Signals are most useful when tracked over time. A single observation is noise. Three months of data reveal the pattern. Use the dashboard below to build that picture.

*(**Note:** This dashboard was first introduced in Chapter 2. Return to Chapter 2 for initial signal overview.)*

Advanced Signal Reading: The Lag Problem

Some trust fractures don't show up immediately. A leader makes a decision in January that breaks trust, but people don't disengage until March.

The reason is patience. People give leaders the benefit of the doubt until the pattern repeats. One inconsistent decision? They assume it's an exception. Two? They start wondering. Three? They conclude: "This is who they are now."

The implication is direct: if you're seeing trust signals in March, the fracture probably started in January. Don't just address the current symptom. Trace back to the original fracture and address that first.

What Strong Leaders Do Differently

Leaders who maintain trust don't wait for annual surveys or formal feedback cycles. They track signals weekly and treat behavioral shifts as data, not noise.

They name signals when they see them. They don't ignore drift or hope it self-corrects. They call it out directly: "I've noticed [signal]. What's happening?" That naming alone often surfaces the fracture before it deepens.

They act within 72 hours. Once a signal is visible, they don't wait to gather more data. They address it immediately. Delay is its own signal, and teams read it clearly.

They ask their team to help them see. The most effective leaders build explicit feedback loops: "If you see me breaking trust, tell me within 72 hours, not six months from now." That request is not a form of weakness. It's a guardrail. For leaders who want to accelerate this work, a trusted mentor or coach can provide an outside perspective with no stake in the outcome and no history inside the system. The goal is the same whether the feedback comes from your team, mentor, or coach: to see the signals before they become fractures.

Your System Check:

- *Look at the eight signals. Which one are you seeing right now?*
- *What will you name and address in the next 72 hours?*

CHAPTER 12: THE 72-HOUR REPAIR PROTOCOL™

"The fracture doesn't define you. The next 72 hours does." —Gearl Loden

Trust breaks quietly. It can be repaired quickly but only if you act before the narrative hardens.

The longer a trust fracture goes unaddressed, the harder repair becomes. Address it within 72 hours, and the path back is clear. Wait 72 days, and you're no longer repairing a moment; you're rebuilding a pattern. Speed matters not for its own sake, but because trust narratives harden on a predictable timeline.

The 72-Hour Repair Protocol™ is designed for fast, targeted trust repair.

Why 72 Hours?

The window matters because trust narratives move on a predictable timeline. Understanding where your team is in that timeline determines what kind of repair is still possible.

Window	What's Happening
Hours 1–24	The fracture is fresh. People are still processing. Conclusions haven't hardened yet.
Hours 25–48	Narratives begin forming. "This is who they are." "I should have known." The story is still soft, but it's moving.
Hours 49–72	The narrative solidifies. People tell others. The story spreads. Repair is still possible, but only if you act now.
After 72 Hours	The narrative is entrenched. Repair requires more than a conversation. It requires a demonstrated pattern change over weeks.

The Four-Step Protocol

Step 1: Name the Pillar Damaged (Hours 1–12)

Trust fractures aren't vague. They're specific. You didn't "lose trust." You damaged a specific pillar through a specific behavior.

Vague acknowledgment feels performative. Specific naming signals that you understand what you did and why it mattered. There's a difference between "I know I messed up" and "I damaged consistency by changing expectations without explanation." The first is a gesture. The second is a diagnosis.

Ask yourself whether your behavior was unpredictable (Consistency), whether you withheld information or failed to explain (Communication), whether you allowed a system to fail (Competence), whether you overloaded someone or ignored capacity (Care), whether you violated a stated value (Character), whether you left something ambiguous (Clarity), or whether you delayed addressing an issue (Courage). Name the pillar. Be specific.

Step 2: Acknowledge Without Defense (Hours 12–24)

This is where most leaders fail. They acknowledge the mistake and then defend it. The "but" erases the acknowledgement. People hear the defense, not the ownership.

Weak—Includes Defense	Strong—Clean Ownership
"I know I should have told you sooner, but I didn't have all the information yet, and I didn't want to create unnecessary worry."	*"I should have told you sooner. I didn't. That created uncertainty and eroded trust. I own it completely."*

No "but." No explanation. No justification. Defensiveness signals that you don't actually believe you were wrong, and teams hear that signal clearly even when the words say otherwise.

IMMEDIATE ACTION

"I [specific behavior]. That damaged [specific pillar]. That was wrong. I own it." Then stop. Don't add caveats.

Step 3: Clarify the Standard (Hours 24–48)

Acknowledgment alone doesn't repair trust. People need to know what you'll do differently, not vague promises but specific behavioral standards they can observe and hold you to.

Vague Promise	Observable Standard
"I'll communicate better going forward." "I'll be more consistent."	*"Going forward, if I know a decision is coming within two weeks, I'll tell you, even if I don't have final details yet." "Going forward, if I change expectations, I'll explain why in the same conversation."*

Apply a simple test: can someone observe whether you're following the standard? If not, it's too vague to rebuild on.

Words repair trust temporarily. Behavior repairs it permanently.

Step 4: Take Visible Action (Hours 48–72)

You must take visible action within 72 hours that demonstrates the new standard, not just announce it.

Visibility is not self-congratulation. It's accountability made observable. When teams see the change happening, rather than just hearing about it, they update their trust calculation. The standard becomes real because you made it real.

IMMEDIATE ACTION

Find an issue that reflects the standard you just committed to and address it within 72 hours. Then tell your team, "I committed to [standard]. Here's what I did this week: [specific action]."

The Full Protocol in Action

The following scenario walks all four steps through a single trust fracture.

Most trust breaks aren't dramatic. They're managerial. You start to notice that standards aren't being enforced consistently. High performers compensate. The team gets cautious. The leader doesn't realize the signal they're sending until the cost shows up in morale, speed, and results.

That's how a leader begins to lose trust in both directions: with the team they lead and with the leaders above them, not because they have a challenging employee issue, but because they let it drift. The supervisor isn't looking for perfection. They're looking for evidence that you will name the issue, hold the standard, and protect the system before the system pays for your delay.

Here is how the protocol works inside a real leadership moment.

The Fracture: I delayed addressing a performance gap for six weeks. High performers noticed. Trust in my willingness to hold standards eroded.

Hours 1–12—Name the Pillar

"I delayed a Courage conversation. That signaled standards were negotiable."

Hours 12–24—Acknowledge Without Defense

"I need to own a mistake. I saw a performance gap impacting outcomes for several weeks. I didn't address it. That's on me. It created an extra load for others and weakened confidence that I'll hold the line. I'm not blaming the person or the situation. I waited. I shouldn't have."

Hours 24–48—Clarify the Standard

"Here's the standard I'm setting for myself: when I see a performance gap that affects the work, I address it within 72 hours."

Hours 48–72—Take Visible Action

"I've already scheduled the conversation and initiated the appropriate next steps. I won't share more than you need for oversight, but I will keep you informed on outcomes and timelines. If you see me drifting again, I want you to call it early. If documentation is required, I will begin it within the same 72-hour window."

Trust begins to repair, not because of the apology, but because the behavior changed visibly and on time.

Step 5: Rebuild Through Pattern: When You Miss the 72-Hour Repair Protocol™ Window

The protocol still works after 72 hours, but the timeline changes.

If you're within 30 days, follow all four steps and add a fifth: rebuild through pattern. You can't repair it with one action. You need to demonstrate the new standard repeatedly across 30 days and sometimes longer before the team recalibrates its trust.

If you're past 30 days, you're beyond fast repair. Use the 90-Day Trust Build™ described in Chapter 16. The fracture is no longer a single incident; it's a documented pattern. Repair requires a longer runway.

Common Mistakes in Repair

Mistake 1: Over-Apologizing

Some leaders apologize excessively, cycling through guilt, self-criticism, and reassurance in ways that center on their own feelings rather than the team's experience. Over-apology signals emotional dysregulation, not accountability. It asks the team to manage the leader's discomfort rather than receive a clean repair.

Acknowledge it once, clearly, then move to action.

Mistake 2: Asking for Forgiveness

"I hope you can forgive me" puts the burden on the other person. It makes the repair contingent on their emotional response rather than on your behavioral change. The team didn't create the fracture. Don't hand them the work of closing it.

Don't ask for forgiveness. Commit to change. "I'm changing [behavior]. You'll see it starting [date]." That's a repair. A request for forgiveness is a performance.

Mistake 3: Waiting for Trust to Return

Repair doesn't happen passively. You can't acknowledge a mistake and then wait for trust to drift back. Trust was broken through behavior. It returns through behavior, visible and repeated, and on the timeline you named.

Actively rebuild. If you said you would demonstrate the standard within 72 hours, demonstrate it within 72 hours. The team is watching the clock, even if they're not saying so.

The Repair Ledger

After using the protocol, track your progress across four weeks. The ledger isn't a performance review; it's a discipline. It keeps you honest about whether repair is actually happening or whether you've completed the steps and moved on.

Period	The Repair Ledger	Yes / No
Week 1	Did I demonstrate the new standard at least once?	
Week 2	Did I demonstrate it again?	
Week 3	Did the team notice the change?	
Week 4	Is the signal that triggered repair gone?	

If all four checks are yes, the repair is working. If any check is no, diagnose which step failed and return to it. Repair isn't a single event. It's a sequence that holds.

Your System Check:

- *What trust fracture happened in the last 72 hours?*
- *Which pillar did you damage?*
- *What will you acknowledge and change within 72 hours?*

PART THREE—RUNNING THE SYSTEM: QUICK REFERENCE

The three tools in Part Three work as a system. The Leadership Ledger™ tracks where the trust system stands; run it weekly. Reading the Signals (Chapter 11) gives you early detection before fractures deepen. The 72-Hour Repair Protocol™ gives you a fast, targeted response when a fracture occurs. Run all three simultaneously: the Ledger prevents drift, the Signals catch what the Ledger misses, and the Repair Protocol closes what the Signals reveal.

PART FOUR—WHEN TRUST BREAKS

CHAPTER 13: THE FIVE FAILURE MODES

"Trust doesn't break randomly. It breaks along predictable lines that most leaders never learned to read." —Gearl Loden

Trust doesn't break randomly. It breaks along five predictable patterns. Most leaders make the same mistakes, not because they're incompetent, but because these patterns are counterintuitive. What feels like good leadership often erodes trust. Building trust can feel uncomfortable. Over more than two decades leading teams and coaching executives through trust failures, I've seen the same five patterns repeat across industries, sectors, and leadership levels. The context changes, but the patterns don't.

This chapter identifies each failure mode, explains why leaders fall into it, and provides a concrete path out.

Failure Mode 1: Verification Masquerading as Accountability

The Leader Thinks	The Team Experiences
"I'm ensuring quality."	*"They don't trust us anymore."*

A leader loses trust in an outcome, so they start checking the work they used to trust. Here's how it starts. Someone misses a deadline, delivers subpar work, or makes a visible mistake. The leader thinks, I can't let that happen again. So they add oversight. They require approval for decisions that used to be delegated. They review work before it's finalized. They ask for status updates multiple times per week. Each step feels reasonable. Taken together, they send an unmistakable signal: I don't believe you can do this.

Verification doesn't build capability. It builds dependency. High performers feel micromanaged and disengage, not loudly, but quietly, which is worse. They stop bringing their best thinking because they know it will be second-guessed anyway. Low performers don't improve. They add documentation to satisfy oversight. The capability gap that triggered the verification in the first place remains unaddressed, now buried under a layer of processes.

THE FIX

Address the gap, not the symptom. If there's a performance issue, name it directly instead of adding oversight: 'Your last three reports had errors in the data analysis section. Here's the standard I need you to meet. Here's the support I'll provide coaching on the methodology and a peer review process. Here's the timeline: 30 days. After that, I trust you to own this again.' That's accountability. Verification addresses the symptom, and the symptom always returns.

Failure Mode 2: Inconsistency Under Pressure

The Leader Thinks	The Team Experiences
"I'm adapting to the crisis."	*"We don't know what to expect anymore."*

A leader operates consistently under normal conditions but becomes unpredictable under pressure. Pressure changes leader behavior in ways that feel justified from the inside but look erratic from the outside. When budgets get tight, a leader stops explaining every decision; it saves time and reduces questions. When deadlines compress, they check the work they used to trust. When pressure increases, they delay non-urgent conversations. Each shift feels strategic, but the team doesn't see strategy. They see a leader whose behavior has become unpredictable. And unpredictability is the opposite of consistency.

Here's what most leaders miss: consistency under normal conditions doesn't build trust. Consistency under pressure builds trust. Anyone can hold a standard when it's easy. What defines a leader is whether the standard holds when it's costly. If your behavior changes when the stakes are high, people conclude that the values only matter when things are comfortable. That conclusion, once drawn, is extraordinarily difficult to reverse.

THE FIX

Narrate the pressure explicitly. When pressure forces you to operate differently, say so: "I know I'm asking more questions than usual. That's not a lack of trust; it's higher stakes. This will return to normal after we close this budget cycle." Or, even better, hold the standard when it's expensive to do so. "I know this deadline is tight, but we're not skipping the review process. Quality matters more than speed." That single sentence, spoken under real pressure, deposits more trust than six months of calm consistency. Trust is built in pressure, not comfort.

Trust isn't built in comfort.
It holds or breaks under pressure.

Failure Mode 3: Silence Disguised as Protection

The Leader Thinks	The Team Experiences
"I don't want to alarm them until I have all the facts."	*"They're hiding something."*

A leader withholds information to "protect" people from worry. This failure mode is seductive because the motives are good. Bad news emerges: layoffs, budget cuts, and a strategic shift that will affect everyone. The leader thinks, "I'll wait until I can share a complete picture." Sharing partial information will just cause panic. So they stay silent, and in that silence, something predictable happens. People sense that something is wrong. They always do. Human beings are remarkably attuned to shifts in tone, behavior, and information flow. When leaders go quiet, teams don't relax into the silence. They fill it. Rumors spread. Anxiety compounds. People create worst-case narratives because worst-case narratives feel safer than the unknown. Silence is just a void.

THE FIX
Communicate before you're ready. You don't need all the facts to say, "This situation is developing. Here's what I know so far: [facts]. Here's what I don't know yet: [gaps]. Here's when I'll have more information: [timeline]." That's not panic-inducing. That's leadership. The vacuum you're trying to prevent by staying silent is already being filled, just not by you.

Failure Mode 4: Avoidance Framed as Patience

The Leader Thinks	The Team Experiences
"I'll give them more time to improve."	*"Leadership won't address the problem."*

A leader delays a hard conversation, telling themselves they're being patient. This is the most common failure mode in coaching. A performance issue emerges. The leader notices it, but the conversation feels uncomfortable, so they delay. They tell themselves they'll wait until the next review cycle, or see if it improves on its own, or find the right moment. Weeks turn into months. The issue compounds.

Here's the damage that leaders consistently underestimate: every day you delay, your high performers are watching. They see the performance gap. They see that you see it. They're concluding that standards don't matter, effort is optional, and leadership won't protect them from carrying others. The math is brutal. A delayed conversation costs you trust with your best people to avoid discomfort with one person. You're trading the commitment of many for the comfort of one, and the person you're "protecting" isn't even being helped. They're being denied the feedback they need to grow.

THE FIX

Apply the 72-hour standard. Address performance issues within 72 hours of noticing them, not at the annual review, not "when the time is right." Within 72 hours. This doesn't mean the full conversation has to happen in 72 hours. It means you initiate. You name it. You open the door. Delayed courage is not patience. It's abdication.

Failure Mode 5: Treating Trust as Sentiment, Not Structure

The Leader Thinks	The Team Experiences
"If people feel valued, trust will follow."	*"We do retreats and surveys, but nothing changes."*

A leader believes trust is built through team-building activities, declarations, and positive culture initiatives. Trust isn't about feelings. It's about behavior. I've worked with leaders who invest heavily in retreats, recognition programs, and culture surveys. These aren't bad things; but they don't build trust, at least not the load-bearing kind. You can take your team to the most meaningful retreat of their careers; and if you come back on Monday and make an inconsistent decision, withhold information about a looming change, or avoid a performance conversation everyone knows needs to happen, the retreat means nothing.

People don't trust leaders who make them feel good. They trust leaders whose behavior is predictable, competent, and courageous.

THE INFRASTRUCTURE SHIFT

Stop investing in trust-building activities and start investing in trust-building systems. Utilize consistent decision-making frameworks so people know how decisions get made. Incorporate transparent communication processes so information flows before rumors do. Invest in development systems so competence grows across the organization, not just in pockets. Implement workload tracking so care isn't aspirational. Apply the 72-hour feedback loop so courage is a habit, not an event. Trust is infrastructure, not inspiration.

Diagnosing Which Failure Mode You're Running

Most leaders run two or three of these modes simultaneously. The patterns overlap and reinforce each other. A leader who avoids hard conversations (Mode 4) often withholds information (Mode 3) and becomes inconsistent under the resulting pressure (Mode 2).

Ask yourself honestly: Am I adding oversight instead of addressing capability gaps? Does my behavior change under pressure in ways my team can't predict? Am I withholding information to "protect" people? What conversation have I been delaying for 30 or more days? Am I investing in culture activities instead of trust systems?

Identify which modes are active. Address them systematically, starting with the one causing the most visible damage. Recognizing the pattern is the first step. Changing the behavior, within 72 hours, is where trust actually gets rebuilt.

Your System Check:

- *Which of the five failure modes are you running right now?*
- *What is the most visible damage it's causing, and what will you change within 72 hours?*
- *Where have you been treating activity as a substitute for accountability?*

CHAPTER 14: HOW YOU REPAIR IS WHO YOU ARE

"A trust breach handled with honesty and follow-through often builds more credibility than if the breach never happened."—Gearl Loden

Here's a counterintuitive truth: handled well, a trust breach can strengthen trust more than if the breach never happened.

Most leaders fear trust breaches because they believe trust lost is trust gone forever, that mistakes destroy credibility, and that people will never forget. But that's not how trust works. Trust is strengthened through repair if repair is done well. When a leader notices a fracture, owns it without deflection, changes their behavior visibly, and demonstrates that change repeatedly, they signal something rare: self-awareness, humility, and the kind of discipline that most leaders talk about but few actually practice. Those signals don't just repair trust. They build credibility that didn't exist before the breach.

The Repair Paradox

Teams don't trust leaders who never fail. Perfection is either a performance or a delusion, and people can sense both. What teams trust is the capacity to recover, to see clearly, acknowledge honestly, and change visibly. A leader who has never broken trust is a leader whose resilience has never been tested; but a leader who has broken trust and repaired it well has demonstrated something far more valuable: they've shown they can be trusted not just in good conditions, but after failure. And in organizational life, failure is not a matter of if but when.

What "Handled Well" Actually Means

Leaders often repair poorly. They apologize vaguely: "I'm sorry if I upset anyone." They defend their intent: "But I was trying to help." They promise vaguely: "I'll do better." Then they wait for trust to return passively, as if trust were a stray cat that might wander home on its own. This doesn't repair trust. It prolongs the fracture and often deepens it, because each ineffective attempt teaches the team that the leader either doesn't understand what they broke or can't fix it.

Handled well means four things, in sequence. First, acknowledge specifically, not "I'm sorry if anyone was upset" but "I damaged trust by doing this specific thing." Second, own it without defense, no "buts," no explanations of intent, and no context that softens accountability. Third, change behavior visibly, not just promises, but observable action that people can see and evaluate. Fourth, demonstrate the change repeatedly, not once as a gesture but as a pattern that becomes the new normal. The sequence matters. Leaders who skip steps don't repair; they perform. And teams know the difference.

The Repair Credibility Curve

Trust repair follows a predictable curve. The credibility gained at each phase builds on what came before, which means the leaders who see the greatest return are the ones who stay the course through all four steps.

Phase	Timeline	What's Happening
Phase 1	*Days 1–3*	Acknowledge the breach without defense. Impact is modest but important; people notice that you're aware that something broke.
Phase 2	*First week*	Make a visible behavioral change. People notice: "They're actually doing something different." Credibility begins to build.
Phase 3	*Weeks 2–4*	Demonstrate the change as a pattern. People notice: "This isn't a one-time thing. They've changed." Credibility accelerates.
Phase 4	*Months 2–3*	The new behavior becomes integrated. People notice: "This is just how they lead now." Credibility often exceeds where you started.

The Three Levels of Repair

Not all trust breaches are equal. The depth of the fracture determines the repair approach. Applying a 72-hour conversation to a systemic breach won't work. Neither will a 90-day protocol for a single incident. Matching the repair to the level of damage is how leaders avoid both underreacting and overcomplicating.

Level	What It Looks Like	Repair Approach	Timeline
Micro-Fracture	A single incident, a decision made without consultation, a moment of frustration that broke trust.	*72-Hour Repair Protocol (Ch. 12)*	1–2 weeks
Pattern Fracture	Repeated behavior, consistently late to commitments, avoiding hard conversations for months.	*30-day pattern change: public acknowledgment, visible shift, enough repetition to be believed.*	4–8 weeks
Systemic Fracture	Multiple pillars broken over an extended period, and damage spread across the team or organization.	*90-Day Trust Build*™ *(Ch. 16)*	3–6 months

Why Some Repairs Fail

Most repair attempts fail for three reasons. Recognizing them is the first step. Changing the behavior is the only one that counts.

Apology Without Change

The leader apologizes, promises to do better, then repeats the same behavior. People learn quickly: apologies are performative; behavior won't change. The fix is simple but hard: don't apologize twice for the same thing. Fix it the first time. A repeated apology is no longer accountability; it's a pattern of its own, and that pattern erodes trust faster than the original fracture did.

A repeated apology is no longer accountability. It's a pattern of its own.

Private Acknowledgment of Public Failure

A leader breaks trust publicly, with an inconsistent decision in a team meeting, a delayed announcement that affects everyone, and unclear communication to the entire organization. Then they apologize privately, in one-on-one conversations. But public fractures require public repair. If only the person you apologized to knows you acknowledged the mistake, the rest of the team still sees the unrepaired fracture. Match the scope of acknowledgment to the scope of the damage. This isn't exposure; it's proportionality.

To be clear: this does not mean calling an all-hands meeting or making a company-wide announcement. It means the acknowledgment reaches the same audience that witnessed the fracture, no wider, and no narrower.

Waiting for Trust to Return

A leader acknowledges their mistake and then waits passively for trust to rebuild. But trust doesn't return automatically. It's rebuilt through visible, repeated behavior change. You have to actively demonstrate the new pattern and narrate it: "I committed to this standard. Here's what I did this week to uphold it." Trust doesn't wander back on its own. You rebuild it brick by brick, and you tell people you're doing it.

The Accountability Announcement

One of the most powerful repair tools available to a leader is the Accountability Announcement. When you've broken trust, you announce publicly what you did wrong, what you're changing, and how people can hold you accountable. It's not a confession. It's a commitment made visible.

> *"I need to acknowledge something. Over the past three months, I've been inconsistent in how I respond to similar situations. That's damaged trust, and I own it.*
>
> *Here's what's changing: I'm creating a decision framework so responses are predictable.*
>
> *Here's how you can hold me accountable: if you see me responding inconsistently, point it out within 48 hours. I'll either explain the difference or acknowledge I was inconsistent."*

This works because it combines three things simultaneously: public acknowledgment that matches the scope of the fracture, a specific change rather than a vague promise, and a mechanism for accountability that gives people real power. This doesn't just repair trust. It strengthens it because the leader has voluntarily made themself accountable in a way that most leaders never do.

LEADERSHIP IN PRACTICE: WHEN REPAIR BECAME THE DEFINING CREDENTIAL

The story didn't start with a crisis. It started with a pattern, one that a founder I coached had been running for nearly a year without fully seeing it. He was the CEO of a mid-size SaaS company that had just completed a merger. Technically strong, operationally sharp, and genuinely invested in his team. He had built the company from twelve people to nearly one hundred, and he still led the way he had when the team fit around one conference table.

That instinct, which had been one of his greatest strengths, had quietly become his most significant trust problem.

When something went sideways in the business, he moved in close. Not to micromanage, but to fix. He would rewrite the messaging, redirect the product decision, and restructure the approach. From where he sat, he was protecting the company from costly mistakes during a critical integration period. From where his leadership team sat, he was signaling that he didn't trust them to lead.

By the time he brought this to our coaching sessions, two of his senior leaders, both inherited from the acquired company, had become disengaged. One had begun quietly exploring other opportunities. He hadn't connected the dots yet. He thought the disengagement was about merger friction, cultural adjustment, and the natural turbulence of integration. He kept offering more involvement and couldn't understand why the response kept cooling.

We ran the Trust Audit™

Competence was his highest score. Not because he wasn't capable; he was one of the sharpest operators I've coached. It scored high because the way he expressed competence had become the organization's greatest source of friction. He was solving problems his leaders needed to solve themselves. He was removing the challenge alongside the risk. His team didn't feel trusted to lead. They felt managed.

This is where leaders often make their first mistake. When he understood what the data was showing, his instinct was to pull back entirely, to stop engaging, to create distance as a form of repair. I had to slow that down.

Pulling back without naming why would have created a different trust problem. His team would have experienced it as withdrawal, not respect. And withdrawal, sudden and unexplained, sends its own signal: something is wrong, and no one will say what it is.

Instead, he named it.

In a meeting with his senior leadership team, he said this: "I want to acknowledge something I've been getting wrong. I've been stepping into your work in ways I intended as support, and you've experienced them as second-guessing. I've been solving problems you were capable of solving, and in doing that, I've signaled that I don't trust your judgment. That was a mistake. I own it. Here's what changes: I will not step in unless you ask me to. And if I see something I'm concerned about, I'll ask a question before I offer a solution. Starting now."

The room was quiet for a moment.

Then one of the acquired company's leaders, the one who had been quietly looking for an exit, said something he hadn't expected:

"That's the first time anyone at the executive level has said something like that to a team I have worked on."

Not "it's okay." Not "don't worry about it." Because acknowledgment, specific, undefended, and forward-facing, is rare enough in organizational life that when it arrives, people don't just notice it. They remember it.

Over the following six weeks, he held the new standard under conditions that tested it directly. A product decision surfaced that he had strong opinions about. His instinct fired immediately. He wanted to redirect it. Instead, he sent a single message to the product lead: "I have a perspective on this. I'm not stepping in, but I'm available if you want to think it through." The product lead handled it effectively.

By week eight, the leader who had been looking for an exit withdrew from the process. Not because everything was resolved, the integration still had real friction. But because the relationship had changed. The team no longer needed to manage the CEO's attention. They could lead.

Twelve months later, when the company faced a difficult platform migration that required cross-functional alignment across both legacy teams, those same leaders drove it. They brought the CEO in, not because they were required to, but because they trusted him to contribute without taking over. That's what repair that holds looks like.

Here is what I want you to notice about that story and about what made the repair credible rather than performative.

He didn't apologize for being capable. He apologized for the form his capability had taken. That distinction matters. Vague accountability dilutes the repair. Specific accountability, "I stepped in when I should have stayed back, and here's the standard going forward," makes it real.

He held the new standard when it was uncomfortable, when his instinct said move in and the discipline said wait. That repetition, visible and sustained, is what converted acknowledgment into credibility.

And critically, the credibility he built after the repair exceeded what existed before it. His team now had evidence they didn't have before the breach, evidence that he could see his own blind spots, own them publicly, and change visibly. That's a more durable form of trust than anything he could have built by simply not making the mistake.

The repair didn't just restore what was there. It built something that wasn't.

That is the repair paradox made real. A leader who breaks trust, repairs it well, and holds the new standard has demonstrated something more valuable: that they can be trusted not just in good conditions, but after failure.

And in organizational life, failure is not a matter of if. It is always a matter of when.

Your System Check:

- *Think about a trust fracture you caused in the last 90 days. Did you repair it well, acknowledge specifically, change visibly, and demonstrate repeatedly?*
- *Or did you apologize and wait for trust to return?*
- *If the latter, what will you do differently this week?*
- *The repair in the story above exceeded pre-breach trust. Where in your current leadership context is there a fracture that, handled well, could become your defining credential?*

CHAPTER 15: TRUST AS LEGACY

"Personal trust evaporates when you leave. Systemic trust is what remains."
—Gearl Loden

Most leaders measure success by outcomes: revenue growth, project completion, awards won, and promotions earned. These matter, but outcomes fade. What remains after you leave is trust, not the trust people had in you while you were there but the trust they maintain in the systems, standards, and culture you built. That distinction is the difference between a leader people remember fondly and a leader whose impact endures. When a leader exits an organization, only three things persist. All three are built or broken through trust.

From the Coaching Room

I didn't start my career thinking about legacy. I started thinking about accountability. In my early years as a leader, I felt the weight of it constantly, the belief that I had to know everything because I was responsible for everything. That belief wasn't wrong. But it was incomplete. It kept me at the center of every decision, every crisis, every outcome. And while that felt like leadership at the time, it was actually a ceiling, one I had built for myself and, without realizing it, for everyone around me.

As I matured as a leader and moved into larger organizations and more complex roles, something shifted. I discovered that the most effective thing I could do wasn't to be the answer; it was to build the people and systems that didn't need me to be. That realization changed how I led. I started focusing heavily on developing others, building leadership pipelines, investing in succession planning, and honing my own skills as a coach. The question I asked changed from "How do I handle this?" to "How do I build a team and culture where this gets handled well, whether I'm here or not?"

That shift didn't happen overnight. It came through years of watching what worked and what didn't, through leading teams that thrived because they had been invested in, and inheriting teams that had been managed but never truly developed. The pattern was always the same. Where leaders had built capacity in others, the organization held steady under pressure. Where leaders had hoarded decision-making authority, even well-run organizations faltered the moment the leader stepped away. The difference was never talent. It was always trust, whether the systems in place had been designed to grow it or simply assume it.

It also came through coaching. Working alongside other leaders, watching them navigate political complexity, organizational resistance, and their own blind spots, sharpened something I couldn't have developed alone. Coaching taught me that the frameworks leaders need aren't motivational. They're structural. Leaders don't fail because they lack passion or intelligence. They fail because they lack systems that translate their values into consistent, visible behavior across every level of the organization. That insight became the backbone of everything I now teach.

That shift also demanded the development of systems, not as bureaucratic infrastructure but as expressions of what we believed. The systems I put in place, and now help others build, are anchored on a foundational belief: our people are our greatest resource. For them to thrive, they need high levels of trust, a clear vision and mission, robust systems, and effective implementation. When those four conditions are present together, trust rises and your people thrive. Performance follows. And the organization can sustain both long after any single leader has gone. I've seen this hold across industries, across organizational size, and across wildly different leadership styles. The variables change. The principle doesn't.

Trust doesn't sustain itself on belief alone. It has to be structurally embedded. For leaders who want to maintain high levels of trust over time, the work extends into every operational layer of the organization: long-range planning, policy development, hiring processes, onboarding, ongoing training, and board development. Each of these must be centered around developing, sustaining, and growing a culture rooted in trust. This isn't optional work that sits alongside leadership. It is leadership. The hiring process either signals what you value or contradicts it. Onboarding either begins the trust relationship or delays it. Board development either reinforces organizational alignment or introduces fractures that ripple downward. Authentic organizational trust isn't a byproduct of good intentions. It's the result of baking the seven pillars into everything you do, not as an initiative but as an operating standard. Systemic trust is the only kind that outlasts you.

Systems, Standards, and Stories: What Each of Those Three Things Requires

Each of the three things a leader leaves behind, systems, standards, and stories, either holds without them or reveals what was never truly built.

What Remains	The Leadership Question
Systems	The processes, structures, and infrastructure you built. The question: Do they work without you, or do they collapse when you leave? A system that depends on a single person isn't a system. It's a dependency.
Standards	The expectations you held and enforced. The question: Do people maintain them after you leave, or do they erode immediately? Standards that only hold because of one leader's presence were never really standards. They were personal preferences backed by positional authority.
Stories	The narratives people tell about your leadership. What do they say you valued? What do they say you tolerated? Stories are the longest-lasting element of legacy because they shape how the next generation of leaders thinks about what's possible and what's expected.

Personal Trust vs. Systemic Trust

Most leaders build personal trust in themselves as individuals. This kind of trust feels good, and it should. But personal trust has a fatal flaw: it evaporates when the leader leaves.

Systemic trust endures. Personal trust is a leadership dependency. Systemic trust is a leadership legacy. The difference shows up most clearly in the language teams use.

Personal Trust	Systemic Trust
"I trust them to make the right call."	"The decision framework is clear; anyone can apply it."
"They always have our back."	"Standards are enforced consistently, regardless of who's leading."
"I know they'll handle it."	"The culture protects people's capacity, even when leadership changes."
Evaporates when the leader leaves.	Endures after the leader leaves.

From Personal to Systemic: The Pillar Legacy Map

The Exit Test reveals where the gaps are. This table shows what it means to close them and what legacy trust looks like, pillar by pillar.

Pillar	Personal	Systemic
Character	People trust your values.	Values are embedded in hiring criteria, decision standards, and cultural expectations, regardless of who leads.
Consistency	People trust your predictability.	Decision frameworks are documented and applied consistently by all leaders in the organization.
Communication	People trust your transparency.	Communication systems create clarity regardless of who is communicating or what their personal style is.
Competence	People trust your capability.	Processes and systems work reliably without depending on any single person's skill or presence.
Care	People trust that you protect them.	Workload standards are structural, enforced by culture and policy, and not dependent on a caring leader's vigilance.
Clarity	People trust your honesty.	Truth-telling is a systemic expectation. The culture demands and protects it, regardless of who's in the room.
Courage	People trust you to have hard conversations.	Hard conversation norms are built into culture. People at every level have the skills and safety to address issues without waiting for leadership.

Most leaders can look at this table and identify the pattern clearly. Some pillars you've built systemically. Others you're still carrying personally.

The question isn't judgment; it's stewardship. What would it take to systematize the ones you're still holding alone?

Building Legacy Trust

Three strategies separate leaders who leave a legacy from those who leave a vacancy.

Document Decision Frameworks

Don't just make good decisions. Document how you make them. Instead of "I approved the budget increase because it felt right," document the criteria: it aligns with strategic priority two, projected ROI is three-to-one within 18 months, risk is contained to a single department, and the team can execute. Now, anyone can apply that framework. Your decision-making outlasts you.

Enforce Standards Through Others

Don't be the only person who holds standards. When you notice a standard slipping, resist the urge to address it personally every time. Coach someone else to address it. This feels slower at the moment, but it means that when you leave, that person continues enforcing the standard. You've replicated your commitment, not just your compliance. There's a significant difference between the two.

Narrate the "Why" Behind Culture

Culture isn't what you say in meetings. It's the stories people tell when you're not there. So narrate intentionally: "We hold this standard because consistent behavior builds trust faster than any amount of talent." "We address issues within 72 hours because delay is a withdrawal from the Leadership Ledger™." When you narrate the why, people internalize it. It becomes culture, not just policy. And culture is what persists.

Sometimes, What Remains Is the Story

The first example I shared shows what legacy trust looks like when systems hold. But I want to share a second story, because not every legacy plays out that way. And this lesson may be the most important one in the chapter.

I worked with a seasoned leader who was recruited to a community navigating significant change. The board that hired her could see clearly that she was the person they needed, someone who could set the stage for long-term success as their community evolved, and they were right.

She built her leadership on every pillar in this framework. She built relationships grounded in character. She was consistent. She communicated with transparency. She built systems. She protected her people. She told the truth even when it was uncomfortable, and she had hard conversations when they needed to happen. Within just a few years, she was being recognized nationally, not just for the performance results her organization had achieved, but also for the culture of trust she had built in the process. And then the politics shifted.

There were power brokers in her community who didn't like the direction things were heading. They were comfortable with how things had been and were willing to work against change to get back to it. They couldn't undo what she had built overnight, so they did it the only way they could, slowly, patiently, replacing her board one seat at a time.

She saw it happening. And she kept leading the same way she always had, using every pillar, right up until the end. When the odds were clearly stacked against her, and she recognized that continued conflict would cost the organization more than her departure, she took the high road. She stepped aside because she cared more about the long-term health of the organization than about holding onto the seat.

Today, she continues to thrive. She is still remembered, by the vast majority of people in that community, as one of the most dynamic leaders they have ever had. Not because of politics. Not because of the people who worked against her. Because of how she led, and because of how she left.

The lesson I want you to take from this: you can do everything right. You can hit the numbers the world considers meaningful. You can build trust at every level of your organization. And still, at times, things simply will not work out. Power brokers are real. Politics is real. Boards change.

But here is what I know from decades of watching leaders at their best and at their hardest: how you finish is part of the story. The decision to lead with dignity until the last day, to protect the organization's future even at personal cost, and to model the pillars when it is hardest to do so, that is the legacy.

The Leadership Succession Test

The ultimate test of legacy trust is how your team responds when your successor arrives. The words they use tell you everything about what you actually built.

What the Team Says

Weak Legacy

"Finally, someone new. Maybe they'll fix things."
You built dependency, not systems.

Neutral Legacy

"Let's see what they do."
You built performance but not culture.

Strong Legacy
"Our systems are strong. We're excited to see how our new leader builds on them."
You built systemic trust, the kind that outlasts you.

Trust as Stewardship

Leadership is stewardship. You inherit systems someone else built. You improve them. And you hand them to the next leader, stronger, ideally, than you found them.

The stewardship question is simple: Will the next leader inherit stronger systems, standards, and culture than you did? If yes, you've built legacy trust. If not, you've extracted value without reinvesting it.

After decades in the chair, the question that matters most to me isn't what I accomplished. It's what remains. Are the systems strong enough to hold without me? Are the standards internalized deeply enough to persist? Will the stories people tell reflect not just what I did, but why I did it? Those are the only measures of legacy that don't fade.

Your System Check:

- ☐ *Would values still be held under pressure? (Character)*
- ☐ *Would decisions still get made predictably? (Consistency)*
- ☐ *Would communication still flow clearly? (Communication)*
- ☐ *Would systems still work reliably? (Competence)*
- ☐ *Would workload still be protected? (Care)*
- ☐ *Would truth still move faster than rumor? (Clarity)*
- ☐ *Would hard conversations still happen within 72 hours? (Courage)*

I want to close this chapter with something beyond the systems and the Exit Test, something the framework alone can't capture.

There are leaders who do everything right, who hit the numbers, who build trust at every level of their organization, and who still face the moment when politics shift, boards change, or external forces create an outcome that no good leadership can prevent. I have watched leaders navigate that moment. What they leave behind in how they exit, with dignity, with care for the organization's future, and with the pillars intact even when personal stakes are highest, that is also legacy. The decision to protect what you built even when you cannot stay to see it, that is trust as its deepest act of service.

Trust as a legacy isn't only about the systems you leave behind. It's about who you were on the way out the door.

CHAPTER 16: THE 90-DAY TRUST BUILD™

"You don't need 90 days to build trust. You need 90 days of the same behavior."

—Gearl Loden

This book has given you the architecture of trust, the seven pillars, the tools to read them, the protocols to repair individual fractures, and the principles to build them into something that outlasts you. Chapter 16 is where you put all of it into motion when the situation is real.

Not every trust challenge requires 90 days. Many can be addressed with the 72-Hour Repair Protocol™ from Chapter 12, the failure mode diagnostics from Chapter 13, or a focused repair from Chapter 14. But when trust is systemically fractured, when multiple pillars have broken over months, when signals are compounding, when execution has slowed, and turnover is rising, a 72-hour repair won't hold. The damage is too serious and too broad. What you need is a structured rebuild. That's what this chapter gives you.

When to Use This Framework

Use this framework when the conditions below are present. The more of these you recognize, the more urgent the rebuild.

Indicator	Condition
Pillar breakdown	Three or more pillars scored "broken" in your Trust Audit™
Duration	Trust drift has been occurring for six months or longer
Signal volume	Multiple trust fracture signals are appearing across different pillars simultaneously
Turnover	Team turnover is increasing without an obvious cause
Execution	Execution has slowed significantly despite no process changes

The Three-Phase Structure

The 90-Day Trust Build™ moves through three phases, each with a distinct goal. Skipping a phase doesn't accelerate the rebuild; it guarantees its failure.

Phase	Timeline	Goal	Focus
Phase 1	Days 1–30	Stabilize	Stop the bleeding. Address the most urgent fracture. Demonstrate that change is possible.
Phase 2	Days 31–60	Strengthen	Test whether the change holds under pressure. Trust rebuilt in calm conditions doesn't count.
Phase 3	Days 61–90	Scale	Add a second pillar. Build feedback loops so trust doesn't drift again after the rebuild.

Phase 1: Stabilize (Days 1–30)

The first phase has one goal: stop the bleeding. You're not trying to rebuild everything. You're trying to address the most urgent fracture and demonstrate that change is possible.

Week 1: Diagnose

Conduct a full Trust Audit™ from Chapter 2. Identify which pillar is most broken, which signal is loudest, and which specific behavior caused the fracture. The output is one pillar to address first. Just one. Don't try to fix everything simultaneously. Leaders who attempt to repair all seven pillars at once diffuse their effort so completely that no single change becomes visible enough to matter.

Week 2: Acknowledge Publicly

This is the hardest part, and it's the part most leaders want to skip; but public acknowledgment is non-negotiable for systemic fractures.

ACKNOWLEDGMENT SCRIPT
"I need to address something that's been broken for some time.
I've damaged trust by [specific behavior]. That broke [specific pillar]. I own that.
Here's what I'm changing: [specific standard].
Here's how you'll know it's working: [observable metric].
Here's the timeline: 30 days."

Name the pillar. Own the behavior. State the standard. Define success. That sequence is not optional.

Weeks 3 and 4: Demonstrate

Visible behavior change repeated consistently. If Consistency is broken, create a decision framework, narrate when you apply it, and explain when you make exceptions. If Communication is broken, commit to proactive updates before people ask, share partial information when full information isn't available, and explain "why" before "what." If Courage is broken, address an issue you've been delaying within 72 hours. The specific actions depend on the specific pillar. But the principle is the same: change must be visible and repeated, not promised and hoped for.

DAY 30 CHECKPOINT

- ☐ *Is the signal reduced or gone?*
- ☐ *Has the team noticed the change?*
- ☐ *Am I demonstrating the standard without reminders?*

If yes to all three, move to Phase 2. If not, extend Phase 1 for another 30 days. There is no shame in needing more time. There is shame in moving on before the first change is solid.

Phase 2: Strengthen (Days 31–60)

Phase 2 tests whether the change holds under pressure. Trust isn't rebuilt in calm conditions. It's rebuilt when stakes are high, and the new behavior still holds.

Weeks 5 and 6: Test the Standard Under Pressure

Intentionally test the new standard when conditions are hard. If you rebuild Consistency, wait for a high-pressure situation, tight deadline, budget cuts, or board scrutiny, and respond consistently with how you'd respond under normal conditions. If you rebuilt Courage, wait for an issue to surface and address it within 72 hours, even though you're busy. Phase 1 showed you can change. Phase 2 shows the change is real.

Weeks 7 and 8: Narrate the Change

People may notice the new behavior but not connect it to your earlier commitment. Narration makes the connection explicit.

NARRATION SCRIPT
"You might have noticed I held the same standard even though we were under deadline pressure this week.
That's intentional. The commitment I made in Week 2 still holds, especially when it's hard."

Narration isn't bragging. It's bridge-building between your intention and your team's perception. Without it, people see behavior and wonder. With it, they see behavior and understand.

DAY 60 CHECKPOINT

- ☐ *Did I maintain the standard without reverting under stress?*
- ☐ *Are the warning signals that indicated breakdown beginning to resolve?*
- ☐ *Is the team operating with more confidence in my leadership?*

If yes, move to Phase 3. If not, extend Phase 2.

Phase 3: Scale (Days 61–90)

Phase 3 adds a second pillar and builds systemic feedback loops so trust doesn't drift again after the rebuild.

Week 9: Add the Second Pillar

Conduct the Trust Audit™ again. Identify which pillar is now most broken, likely the second-worst from Day 1. Follow the same process: acknowledge publicly, state the new standard, demonstrate visibly.

Only two pillars in 90 days. Depth of change matters more than breadth of intention.

Two pillars rebuilt well will always outperform seven pillars rebuilt poorly.

Week 10 Through 12: Build Feedback Loops

Create mechanisms for ongoing trust monitoring: a weekly self-check that takes a few minutes every Friday, a monthly team pulse with two or three direct questions, and a quarterly trust audit using the full framework from Chapter 2. Feedback loops catch drift before it becomes fractured. Without them, the rebuild erodes as soon as attention moves to the next crisis.

DAY 90 CHECKPOINT

- ☐ *Have the two pillars moved from broken to functional?*
- ☐ *Is the team showing significantly fewer signs of the original breakdown?*
- ☐ *Is the team using feedback loops without being prompted?*
- ☐ *Is execution reflecting the trust gains made over 90 days?*

If yes, trust is rebuilding. Continue with the feedback loops and add one additional pillar every 90 days until all seven are strong. The honest timeline for a full systemic rebuild: 12 to 18 months.

If 12 to 18 months sounds like a long time, you're measuring it against the wrong standard. Trust isn't a project with a completion date. It's infrastructure that requires ongoing maintenance. The leaders who sustain the highest levels of trust aren't the ones who fixed it once. They're the ones who never stopped tending to it.

When the 90-Day Trust Build™ Falls Short

Some builds fail. The causes are almost always the same, and they are diagnosable.

Failure Mode	What Happens	The Fix
Scope creep	Trying to fix all seven pillars simultaneously, diffusing effort so no single change becomes visible enough to matter.	Choose one pillar. Only one. Restart there.
Insufficient demonstration	Demonstrating the new behavior once or twice instead of repeating multiple times in 30 days.	Trust is rebuilt through repetition. Volume matters as much as intention.
Silent change	Changing behavior without narrating it, so the team never connects the new pattern to the original commitment.	Narrate explicitly. Make the bridge visible.
Pressure reversion	Holding the standard in calm moments, then reverting under pressure, which tells the team the old behavior was the real one.	Pressure is the test. If you revert, restart Phase 1.

If your building fails, diagnose which of these caused it. Then restart, not from scratch, but from the point of failure. The 90-Day Trust Build™ is a process, not a test. Failure doesn't mean the approach is wrong. It means the execution needs adjustment. That distinction matters.

The 90-Day Trust Build™ in Practice

A superintendent I coached came to me after a difficult stretch. She had inherited a district where trust had been drifting for years before she arrived. The problems weren't dramatic, no single crisis, no headline event. Just gradual erosion: decisions that felt inconsistent, standards that shifted depending on who was asking, issues that surfaced in hallway conversations but never in leadership meetings. By the time she ran the Trust Audit™, four pillars were fractured.

Her instinct was to fix all four simultaneously. I told her to pick one. She chose Consistency because it was the fracture her team felt every day, and because visible improvement there would signal to everyone that change was actually happening.

Week 2, she acknowledged it publicly. Not vaguely, specifically. She named the pattern, owned it without qualification, stated the new standard, and defined what success would look like in 30 days. The room was quiet. Several people told me later it was the first time in years a leader had stood in front of them and said, "I broke something, and here's what I'm going to do about it."

She called me after that meeting. "I thought admitting it would make things worse," she said. "But the room didn't fall apart. It went still, in a way I hadn't felt in that building before. Like people could finally exhale."

That's what real acknowledgment does when a leader means it. It doesn't diminish them. It releases the room.

By Day 60, the language with her team had begun to shift. She told me, "They're not asking me to make every call anymore. They're running things through the framework themselves."

That's precisely what systemic trust sounds like when it starts to take hold.

Eighteen months later, all seven pillars were in the green. Not because she had fixed everything at once. Because she had fixed one thing at a time, completely, with demonstrated proof at every step.

Starting a 90-Day Trust Build™ isn't a sign of failure. It's a sign of a leader serious enough to face what's broken, humble enough to own it publicly, and disciplined enough to demonstrate change until trust is restored.

That combination, self-awareness, accountability, and consistency over time, is what this entire framework is built on.

You've read every pillar. You have the tools. The only thing that remains is the decision to begin.

To see the complete system applied under real pressure, read Appendix D: Trust Under Pressure. The full-system rebuilds documented there show what a 90-Day Trust Build™ looks like when it works and what it costs when leaders wait too long to start.

Your System Check:

- *If you needed to start a 90-Day Trust Build™ tomorrow, which pillar would you address first?*
- *Why that pillar? What specific behavior would you change?*
- *What has prevented you from addressing it until now?*

Conclusion: Building Trust Deliberately

I want to be honest with you about something before we close.

I didn't write this book as an expert looking down at a problem I've solved. I wrote it as someone who has lived inside the same tension you're navigating, who has carried the weight of a team's trust, felt it strain, and had to figure out how to repair what I'd broken while the work kept moving.

I've been the leader who moved too fast. Who confused authority with trust. Who walked into a role with real capability and a solid plan and still watched things fracture because I hadn't earned the right to execute yet. That wasn't a failure of intention. It was a failure of understanding what trust actually requires.

That experience didn't leave me. It shaped every conversation I've had with leaders since, in coaching rooms, in boardrooms, and in quiet one-on-ones after a hard meeting. The details change. The pattern doesn't.

What I Hope You Take From This

What I've tried to give you isn't a system to master. It's a lens to see through, one that puts trust where it belongs: at the center of how you lead, not at the margins of how you feel.

We walked through the seven pillars together, not as ideals to aspire to but as disciplines to practice.

Pillar	What It Demands
Character	Holding values when they're expensive
Consistency	Predictable behavior under pressure
Communication	Reducing uncertainty before it fills with rumor
Competence	Building systems that outlast individual heroics
Care	Protecting capacity, not just feelings
Clarity	Delivering truth faster than speculation
Courage	Acting on what needs addressing despite the discomfort

We also built the tools to implement those disciplines: the Leadership Ledger™, signal reading, the 72-Hour Repair Protocol™, and the 90-Day Trust Build™. Leadership is not a checklist. But when trust is breaking and the pressure is high, having a clear next move matters more than having the right instinct.

The Thing Most Leaders Get Wrong

Most of the leaders I work with aren't struggling because they don't care. They're struggling because they've been taught to measure trust as a feeling, something the team either has or doesn't have, something culture either generates or withholds.

What I've seen over decades of leading teams and coaching is this: the leaders who build the most durable trust aren't the most charismatic or the most vulnerable or the most inspiring. They're the most consistent. The most honest about what's broken. The quickest to name it and change.

They treat trust like the infrastructure it is, something worth maintaining before it fails, not scrambling to repair after it does.

The Choice in Front of You

You're already running a trust system. That's not a metaphor; it's just true. Every leader is. Every day your decisions, your communication, your follow-through, and your silences, all of it is making deposits or withdrawals on behalf of the people who are counting on you.

The question has never been whether you're building or eroding trust. You're always doing one or the other. The question is whether you're doing it *deliberately* or by *default.*

Running Trust by Default	Running Trust Deliberately
React to problems after they surface	Track signals before problems surface
Unable to diagnose where trust is leaking	Know which specific behaviors strengthen each pillar
Treat trust as luck or personality	Diagnose fractures early and repair them quickly
Wait for damage to become visible	Treat trust as infrastructure you actively maintain

You need one honest look and one visible move.

When	The Move
Today	Pull up the Trust Audit™ from Chapter 2. Not to grade yourself, but to see yourself clearly. Which pillar is carrying the most weight right now? Which signal is loudest?
Tomorrow	Name the fracture precisely. The pillar. The behavior. The signal you're seeing. Then say something. To your team if it's a public fracture. To the affected person if it's private. The naming is the first act of repair.
Within 72 Hours	Demonstrate new behavior. State the standard. Make it visible. Then repeat it ten or more times over 30 days. Not as a performance. As proof.

That's the whole launch. Not elegant. Not complicated. Just honest and repeated.

A Letter to the Leader

You finished the book. That means something, but not what you might think.

Finishing a book about trust doesn't make you more trustworthy. Reading about the pillars doesn't strengthen them. Understanding the framework is not the same as running it.

The leaders who get the most from what you've just read are the ones who put it down and immediately feel the weight of something they've been avoiding, a conversation they've delayed, a standard they've let slide, or a signal they've been explaining away. That discomfort isn't a side effect of this work. It's the beginning of it.

So before you move on, I want to ask you something I ask every leader I work with at this stage.

Not which pillar is weakest. Not which tool you'll implement first. Those are good questions, and the framework gives you the language to answer them. But underneath those questions, there's a harder one.

Who is waiting on you?

There is someone on your team, maybe more than one, who has been watching to see if you're going to do the thing you already know needs doing. They haven't said it out loud. They may not even be fully conscious of it. But they're watching. The way people always watch when trust is fragile and the leader has the power to either confirm their doubt or surprise them.

You know who it is. You probably thought of them somewhere in the middle of this book and kept reading.

That person is the answer to the question of where you start. Not the Trust Audit™. Not the 72-Hour Repair Protocol™. Not the Leadership Ledger™. Those tools are real, and they work. But they work best when they're in service of something honest, and the most honest thing you can bring to this framework right now is the name of the person or situation you kept circling back to while you were reading.

Name it. Address it. Within 72 hours.

Not because the protocol says so. Because you already know it's overdue, and every day it stays unaddressed is a day your team is forming conclusions about you based on your silence.

I opened this book by telling you about the season that cost me something. The decision I accelerated. The governance meeting where trust debt went public. The hard realization that intent doesn't travel on its own, that architecture is its superhighway.

I didn't share that story to establish credibility. I shared it because the leaders I most respect aren't the ones who have never made that kind of mistake. They're the ones who looked at it clearly, owned what they had broken, and rebuilt something more durable in its place.

That season didn't just change how I lead. It gave me the reason to build everything you've just read.

You are now holding the same architecture that took me years to develop through success and failure, through trial and error. The pillars. The Ledger. The Sequence. The protocols. The tools to read signals before they become fractures and to repair fractures before they become failures. What you do with them is the only thing that matters now.

That governance meeting didn't end in a room full of cautious people. It ended in a decision to build something that would make the next room different. You've just read what came from that decision. The room you walk into next week, the conversation you've been delaying, and the standard you've been letting slide, those are your governance meetings. The architecture is already in your hands. The only question left is whether you build before it breaks.

The framework gave you the language. The work was always yours.

Close the book. Name the person. Have the conversation.

The architecture is in your hands.
Lead deliberately.
— Gearl Loden

APPENDICES
&
RESOURCES

Appendix A

The Trust Conversation Frame-Framework™

Scripts and Language for Repair Conversations

Trust repair often stalls, not because leaders lack awareness but because they lack language.

Knowing you've broken trust is one thing. Knowing what to say to repair it is another.

This appendix provides six conversation frameworks and scripts for the most common trust repair situations leaders face. Use them as guides, not verbatim scripts. Adapt the language to your style. But preserve the structure, because structure is what separates repair from apology.

How to use this appendix

Identify the trust situation you're facing, go to the matching framework, and adapt the script to your voice. Each framework follows the same four moves: name it, own it, state the change, and ask for engagement, but the entry point and tone shift depending on the situation.

Framework 1: Acknowledgment Without Defense

When to use: You made a mistake that broke trust through inconsistency, avoidance, or poor communication, and the team has noticed.

	THE STRUCTURE
1	Name what you did (or didn't do)
2	Name the impact
3	State what happens next
4	Stop talking

SCRIPT

"I need to address something directly.

Over the past [timeframe], I've [specific behavior]. That's created [specific impact]. I own that.

Here's what's changing: [specific commitment].

You'll see that starting [specific date]."

EXAMPLE—CONSISTENCY BROKEN

"Over the past month, I've been inconsistent in how I've responded to scheduling conflicts, saying yes to some and no to others without explaining why.

That's created confusion about what the standard actually is. I own that.

Here's what's changing: from now on, I'll apply the same criteria to every scheduling request and explain the decision when it's not obvious.

You'll see that starting today."

Avoid This	Why It Fails
"I'm sorry if anyone was upset…"	Shifts blame to their reaction, not your behavior
"But I didn't have all the information…"	The word "but" erases everything before it
"I was trying to help…"	Centers your intent, not their experience

WHY THIS WORKS
✓ No justifications or hedging
✓ Acknowledges impact, not just action
✓ Names a specific, visible commitment with a start date

Framework 2: The Delayed Courage Conversation

When to use: You've been avoiding a hard conversation and need to have it now. The delay itself has cost trust.

	THE STRUCTURE	YOUR SCRIPT
1	Name the delay	
2	Name the cost of the delay	
3	Have the conversation now	
4	Reestablish the standard	

SCRIPT

"I should have had this conversation [timeframe] ago.

By delaying it, I've [specific cost]. I'm addressing it now.

Here's what needs to change: [specific standard].

Here's the support I'll provide: [specific resource].

Here's the timeline: [specific date].

And here's what happens if this doesn't shift: [specific consequence]."

EXAMPLE—PERFORMANCE ISSUE

"I should have had this conversation two months ago.

By delaying it, I've let a performance gap widen and sent a signal that standards are negotiable. I'm addressing it now.

Here's what needs to change: your project delivery needs to meet the agreed timeline without last-minute escalations.

Here's the support I'll provide weekly 15-minute check-ins to surface blockers early.

Here's the timeline: consistent on-time delivery over the next 60 days.

And here's what happens if this doesn't shift: we'll revisit whether this role is the right fit."

Avoid This	Why It Fails
"I've been meaning to talk to you about this..."	Highlights your delay without owning it
"Some people have mentioned..."	Indirect attribution creates paranoia and erodes safety
"I hate having this conversation..."	Centers your discomfort, not their need for clarity

WHY THIS WORKS

✓ Naming the cost of delay builds credibility, not just accountability

✓ Providing support demonstrates care alongside standards

✓ Stating consequences demonstrates courage

Framework 3: The Inconsistency Repair

When to use: You've applied standards unevenly, and people have noticed. The standard itself may be fine; the application wasn't.

	THE STRUCTURE
1	Name the inconsistency specifically
2	Name the correct standard
3	Reapply to it publicly
4	Invite accountability

SCRIPT

"I've realized I've been inconsistent in how I've applied [standard].

Specifically, I [example 1] but not [example 2].

The standard is: [clear statement].

Going forward, here's how this will work: [specific process].

If you see me deviate from this without explanation, I want you to call it out."

EXAMPLE—DEADLINE ENFORCEMENT

"I've realized I've been inconsistent in how I've applied deadline accountability.

I extended the timeline for the marketing deck without consequence but held firm on the finance report deadline.

The standard is that deadlines are firm unless there's a documented blocker surfaced at least 48 hours before the due date.

Going forward, if you need an extension, email me the extension request and propose a new date. If the deadline passes without communication, we'll address it directly.

If you see me deviate from this without explanation, I want you to call it out."

WHY THIS WORKS
✓ Specific examples build credibility because they signal self-awareness
✓ A clear process removes ambiguity about what comes next
✓ Inviting accountability signals you mean it this time

Framework 4: The Withheld Information Recovery

When to use: You delayed communication to wait for complete information, to protect people from worry, or to avoid conflict, and it created distrust instead.

	THE STRUCTURE
1	Acknowledge the gap
2	Explain briefly why you waited (not as justification, as honesty)
3	Share what you should have shared earlier
4	Commit to a new communication standard

SCRIPT

"I should have told you this sooner.

I waited because [brief reason, not justification]. That was a mistake.

Here's what I should have shared earlier: [information].

Going forward, here's my commitment: [specific communication standard]."

EXAMPLE—BUDGET CONSTRAINTS

"I should have told you about the budget constraints two weeks ago.

I waited because I wanted to have a solution before sharing the problem. That was a mistake.

Here's what I should have shared earlier: we're operating at 15% over budget for Q2, which means we need to cut discretionary spending starting next month.

Going forward, my commitment is this: I'll share financial pressure as soon as I see it, even if I don't have the solution yet. You'll hear about constraints early, not late."

WHY THIS WORKS
✓ A brief explanation without justification maintains honesty without excuse-making
✓ Sharing the withheld information demonstrates follow-through on the new standard immediately
✓ A specific forward commitment is more powerful than a general apology

Framework 5: The Competence Gap Conversation

When to use: Someone is in a role they can't execute at the level it requires. The gap is about capability, not effort, and that distinction matters for how you hold it.

	THE STRUCTURE
1	Name the gap specifically
2	Separate capability from character
3	Offer a path forward
4	State the decision timeline

SCRIPT

"I need to talk about [specific responsibility]. Right now, [specific gap].

This isn't about effort or intent; it's about capability in this area.

Here's what I'm seeing: [specific evidence].

Here are the options: [path 1], [path 2].

Here's the timeline for deciding: [specific date].

What questions do you have?"

EXAMPLE—ROLE MISFIT

"I need to talk about project management responsibilities.

Right now, timelines are slipping consistently, and escalations are happening at the last minute instead of early. This isn't about effort or intent; you're working hard. It's about capability in this specific area.

Here's what I'm seeing: three projects in a row have missed deadlines without early warning, and stakeholder communication has been reactive instead of proactive.

Here are the options: we shift you into a senior contributor role where execution is the focus, or we invest in 90 days of intensive project management coaching with weekly check-ins.

Here's the timeline: let's meet again in one week after you've had time to think about what fits.

What questions do you have?"

WHY THIS WORKS
✓ Separating capability from character preserves dignity and keeps the conversation forward-focused
✓ Providing options demonstrates care without lowering the standard
✓ Stating a clear timeline demonstrates the clarity needed for trust to hold

Framework 6: The Self-Trust Recovery Conversation

When to use: You've made repeated mistakes and are doubting your own judgment. Self-trust is eroding, and it's leaking into your leadership. This conversation is internal or with a trusted mentor or peer.

	THE STRUCTURE
1	Name what you're doubting specifically
2	Separate past mistakes from future capability
3	Identify one decision you'll make without second-guessing
4	Make it within 72 hours

INTERNAL SCRIPT

"I've been second-guessing [specific decision type] because of [specific past mistake].

That mistake taught me [specific lesson], but it doesn't mean I can't make sound decisions going forward.

The next time I face [situation], I'm going to [specific action] without checking behind me.

I'm making that decision within 72 hours."

WITH A MENTOR, COACH OR TRUSTED PEER

"I need to process something.

Over the past [timeframe], I've [specific mistakes]. I'm starting to doubt my judgment. I'm second-guessing decisions I used to make confidently.

Help me see if this is a pattern or a rough patch. What are you seeing that I might be missing?

Where do I still have solid judgment, and where do I need to rebuild?"

	THE STRUCTURE
1	Name what you're doubting specifically
2	Separate past mistakes from future capability
3	Identify one decision you'll make without second-guessing

Self-trust is a prerequisite for team trust. You cannot lead clearly from a position of chronic self-doubt. Rebuild it with the same discipline you'd bring to any other trust fracture: name it, own it, act.

Common Mistakes in Trust Conversations

Even with the right framework, these four patterns undermine repair before it begins.

Mistake	What It Sounds Like	The Fix
Apologizing without changing	*I'm sorry I was inconsistent. [Stays inconsistent.]*	Name the change. Then make it visible.
Over-explaining	*I've been inconsistent because the pressure has been significant and the timeline unrealistic..."*	I've been inconsistent. I own that. Full stop.
Deflecting responsibility	*I know I should have communicated sooner, but you didn't ask.*	I should have communicated sooner. That's on me.
Vague commitments	*I'll try to be better about this.*	Here's specifically what I'm doing differently starting today.

When to Seek External Support

Some trust fractures, especially those involving self-trust, benefit from support beyond what this framework provides. Know when to reach further.

Signs You Need External Support	Resources to Seek
Multiple trust fractures in a short timeframe	Executive coach, trusted mentor
Repeating the same mistakes despite awareness	Executive coach, peer accountability partner
Losing confidence in your own judgment	Executive coach, trusted mentor, peer group
Isolation, not talking to anyone about struggles	Professional counselor, trusted mentor

Appendix B

Advanced Trust Diagnostics

Complex Leadership Moments That Test Multiple Pillars

The seven pillars give you a framework. This appendix gives you sharper tools for situations where trust is breaking in complex, layered, or ambiguous ways.

These diagnostics are designed for leaders who have examined their own leadership patterns and need more precision, whether coaching themselves, coaching others, or navigating a multi-layered trust breakdown within a system.

How to use this appendix

Each section presents a complex scenario, a multi-pillar diagnostic, and the highest-leverage leadership move. Use these as coaching prompts, leadership team discussion tools, or solo reflection during a trust breakdown.

Section 1: How the Pillars Interact

Trust rarely breaks along a single pillar. More often, a fracture in one pillar cascades, and misdiagnosing the source leads to the wrong repair. The table below maps common complex scenarios to the pillars most likely implicated.

Scenario	Pillars Implicated
Team stops sharing problems early	Communication, Care, Courage
Experienced people are leaving	Clarity, Character, Consistency
Leader's decisions questioned publicly	Competence, Character, Communication
Standards are ignored across the team	Consistency, Courage, Clarity
A high performer loses motivation	Care, Communication, Clarity
Board or senior leaders lost confidence	Competence, Communication, Character
Culture of silence around real issues	Courage, Care, Communication
Conflict between two high-stakes team members	Clarity, Consistency, Courage

Section 2: Complex Trust Scenarios

The following scenarios reflect the kind of layered trust breakdowns that resist simple diagnosis. Each includes the presenting signal, the deeper diagnostic, and the priority leadership move.

Scenario 1: The Invisible Exodus

When you see it: Your strongest contributors are leaving, not loudly, not in conflict, but quietly. Exit interviews are polite. Retention conversations don't surface real issues.

	THE STRUCTURE
1	Recognize the pattern: quiet departures, polite exits, real reasons surfacing months later
2	Diagnose the root: this is a Clarity-Care failure, not a compensation issue
3	Build a Stay Conversation practice: quarterly 20-minute one-on-ones focused on retention
4	Act on what you hear within 30 days

THE SITUATION

Your strongest contributors are leaving, not loudly, not in conflict, but quietly. Exit interviews are polite. Retention conversations don't surface real issues. You find out the real reason months later through a peer.

DIAGNOSTIC

This is seldom about compensation or workload alone. An invisible exodus is almost always a Clarity-Care failure: people stopped believing the leader has their interests in mind and stopped trusting that honest conversations are safe. The silence in exit interviews signals that the trust is already gone; they've decided not to invest in repairing it.

THE MOVE

Don't wait for exit interviews. Build a Stay Conversation practice: quarterly 20-minute one-on-ones specifically about what would make the person more likely to stay. Ask directly: "What's one thing I could do differently that would make you more likely to stay?" Then act on what you hear within 30 days.

WHY THIS WORKS
✓ Stay Conversations surface problems before they become resignations
✓ Asking directly signals Care—that you want the person, not just the output
✓ Acting within 30 days proves Consistency between words and behavior

Scenario 2: The Public Underminer

When you see it: A well-liked team member is consistently undermining your decisions in informal conversations. Nothing direct, nothing documented, but the pattern is clear.

	THE STRUCTURE
1	Name the pattern specifically: the behavior, not the gossip
2	Diagnose the root: Character-Courage failure on both sides
3	Have a direct conversation within 72 hours

THE SITUATION

A member of your team, well-liked and respected by peers, is consistently undermining your decisions in informal conversations. Nothing direct, nothing documented. But the pattern is clear: every initiative you launch gets quietly relitigated behind closed doors.

DIAGNOSTIC

This is a Character-Courage problem on both sides. The team member is operating outside the agreed communication standard, and the leader's delay in naming it signals either conflict avoidance or uncertainty about standing. Every day the pattern continues, it taxes the trust of everyone who witnesses it.

THE MOVE

Have a direct conversation within 72 hours. Name the pattern specifically, not the gossip, but the behavior. "I've noticed that decisions we make together are being relitigated in other conversations. That creates confusion about what the standard is. I need that to stop." Then state the standard: disagreement happens in the room, not outside it.

WHY THIS WORKS

✓ Naming the behavior (not the gossip) keeps the conversation forward-focused

✓ The 72-hour timeline prevents the pattern from compounding

✓ Stating the standard restores Clarity for the entire team, not just the individual

Scenario 3: The Credibility Cliff

When you see it: You've made a major public commitment, and the delivery has fallen short. The gap between promise and outcome is real and visible.

	THE STRUCTURE
1	Acknowledge the gap publicly, in the same venue where the commitment was made
2	Diagnose the root: Competence-Character fracture. The Competence hit is unavoidable; the Character hit is optional
3	State what happened without blame. State what changes.
4	Give a specific new commitment with accountability built in

THE SITUATION

You've made a major public commitment to your team, your board, or your community, and the delivery has fallen short. The gap between promise and outcome is real and visible.

DIAGNOSTIC

Credibility cliffs are Competence-Character fractures. The Competence hit is unavoidable. The Character hit is optional, determined entirely by how you respond. Leaders who explain, justify, or minimize the gap deepen both failures. Leaders who acknowledge the gap directly and map the path forward arrest the credibility loss and sometimes deepen trust.

THE MOVE

Acknowledge the gap publicly, in the same venue where the commitment was made. State what happened without blame. State what changes. Give a specific new commitment with accountability built in: "I'll update you on progress at [specific date]. If we're not on track, you'll hear it from me first."

WHY THIS WORKS
✓ Public acknowledgment in the same venue signals Character, you're not hiding from the audience that heard the original promise
✓ A new commitment with a date converts apology into accountability
✓ The phrase "you'll hear it from me first" restores Communication trust

Scenario 4: The Trust Inheritance

When you see it: You've stepped into a role where the previous leader broke trust repeatedly. The team is cautious, protective, and slow to engage.

	THE STRUCTURE
1	Name what you're hearing without defensiveness
2	Diagnose the root: Consistency-Care challenge with a long timeline
3	Don't promise a fresh start: promises accelerate skepticism in low-trust environments
4	Be relentlessly consistent for 90 days. Small signals. No surprises.

THE SITUATION

You've stepped into a role where the previous leader broke trust repeatedly, visibly, and in ways that are still felt. The team is cautious, protective, and slow to engage. You're being measured against wounds you didn't cause.

DIAGNOSTIC

This is a Consistency-Care challenge with a long timeline. The previous leader's behavior set an expectation that leadership isn't safe. You don't repair inherited distrust through inspiration or vision; you repair it through predictability. Repetition over time. Signals that align with words.

THE MOVE

Don't promise a fresh start. Promises accelerate skepticism in low-trust environments. Instead, name what you're hearing without defensiveness: "I know trust here has been earned slowly and broken quickly. I'm not asking you to trust me; I'm asking you to watch." Then be relentlessly consistent for 90 days. Small signals. No surprises.

WHY THIS WORKS

✓ "I'm not asking you to trust me; I'm asking you to watch" removes the pressure of premature commitment

✓ 90 days of Consistency is more persuasive than any vision deck

✓ Small signals compound—predictability rebuilds safety faster than inspiration

Scenario 5: The Burnout Blind Spot

When you see it: The numbers are solid. Deliverables are landing. But the pace is unsustainable, and you know it. People are grinding quietly because the culture has rewarded relentless output.

	THE STRUCTURE
1	Name the pace directly, before the collapse
2	Diagnose the root: Care failure disguised as a performance success
3	Make a real change to workload, timeline, or staffing, not a symbolic gesture
4	Build a sustainability signal into the operating rhythm

THE SITUATION

Your team is performing, the numbers are solid, and deliverables are landing. But the pace is unsustainable, and you know it. People are grinding, and they're doing it quietly because the culture has rewarded relentless output.

DIAGNOSTIC

This is a Care failure disguised as a performance success. Leaders who optimize for output without protecting capacity are making a trust withdrawal every week. The team may not name it yet, but they're feeling it. When the collapse comes, it tends to be sudden: a resignation, a health event, a team-wide disengagement that surprises no one except the leader.

THE MOVE

Name the pressure directly before the collapse. "I've been watching the workload, and I'm concerned about sustainability. I want to talk about what we can shift." Then actually shift something. A symbolic gesture won't repair a structural problem. Make a real change to the workload, timeline, or resourcing.

WHY THIS WORKS

✓ Naming the pace before anyone asks signals that you're watching capacity, not just output

✓ A real change (not a symbolic one) proves Care is operational, not performative

✓ The team stops hiding capacity problems; they bring them early because they trust you'll respond

Section 3: Per-Pillar Diagnostic Questions

When to use alongside the Trust Scorecard™ (Appendix C) when a pillar scores fragile or broken and you need deeper precision. These questions work equally well as coaching prompts in one-on-one conversations and leadership team reviews. They are intentionally uncomfortable and are designed to surface what leaders often avoid seeing.

Character—Diagnostic Questions

□ Where am I saying one thing and doing another?

□ What decision did I make in private that I wouldn't want visible?

□ Whose approval am I seeking when I should be making a values-based call?

□ What do I claim to believe that my calendar and budget don't reflect?

Consistency—Diagnostic Questions

□ Where am I applying standards to some people that I'm not applying to others?

□ What decision have I reversed without explaining why?

□ Where does my behavior under pressure differ from my stated values?

□ If someone tracked every decision I made this month, what pattern would they see?

Communication—Diagnostic Questions

□ What do I know that my team doesn't and should?

□ Where am I waiting for complete information before communicating a partial truth?

□ What question is my team afraid to ask me directly?

□ What is being said in hallways that isn't being said to my face?

Competence—Diagnostic Questions

□ Where am I in a role that has outgrown my current skill set?

□ What decision have I been avoiding because I'm not sure I'll get it right?

□ Who on my team is more capable than I am in a critical area, and am I using them well?

□ What system am I running on instinct that should be documented?

Care—Diagnostic Questions

□ Who on my team is struggling and hasn't told me?

□ What request have I ignored or deprioritized that mattered to someone?

□ Where have I protected the work at the expense of the person doing it?

□ When did I last ask someone how they were doing and actually waited for the real answer?

Clarity—Diagnostic Questions

□ What does my team think is the priority right now, and do I know if they're right?

□ What decision am I holding onto that my team could make with the right information?

□ Where am I allowing ambiguity to linger because clarity feels risky?

□ What have I said recently that could be interpreted two ways?

Courage—Diagnostic Questions

□ What conversation am I avoiding that everyone knows I should have?

□ What standard have I let slide because enforcing it is uncomfortable?

□ Where have I let fear of conflict shape a decision that should have been values-based?

□ What is the cost, to the team, to the culture, of my continuing to avoid this?

Section 4: Multi-Pillar Repair Sequencing

When multiple pillars are broken simultaneously, repair sequencing matters. Trying to fix everything at once typically fixes nothing. The following framework helps leaders identify where to start.

Priority	Start Here When…	Why
1	**Character is broken**	No other repair holds without credibility. Character is the foundation.
2	**Consistency is erratic**	Inconsistency undermines every other signal. Even good intent looks manipulative when standards shift.
3	**Communication has broken down**	Silence creates stories. Restore communication.
4	**Competence gaps remain**	Provide systems, training, resources to close the gap that's creating distrust.
5	**Care is absent**	Competence without care creates compliance, not trust. Restore the relationship while you fix the process.
6	**Clarity is absent**	People can't follow a standard they don't understand. Clarity makes every other pillar legible.
7	**Courage is missing**	Everything else can be repaired while courage is developing, but without it, gains will stall.

Appendix C

The Trust Scorecard™

Weekly, Monthly & Quarterly Assessment Tools

The Trust Scorecard™ is a structured self-assessment tool designed to give leaders a clear picture of where their trust system is strong, where it is weakening, and where immediate action is needed.

This is not a performance review. It is a diagnostic, meant to surface what is actually happening in your leadership, not what you hope or intend.

How to use this scorecard

Score each behavior 1–4 based on where you are today, not where you aspire to be. Be precise. Score 3 only if the behavior is typically strong. Score 4 only if it is documented, systematized, and sustained without extra effort.

Complete this assessment alone first. Then compare with a trusted peer or coach. The gaps between what you see and what others see are often more instructive than the scores themselves.

Part 1: Behavioral Assessment

Score each behavior below on a scale of 1–4. Use the descriptions in each column as anchors.

Character

Behavior	1 – Not Present	2 – Emergent	3 – Strong	4 – Systematized	Score
Values alignment	My actions contradict my stated values.	I hold my values sometimes.	My behavior aligns with my values consistently.	My values are embedded in decisions, systems, and culture.	
Transparency under pressure	I hide the truth when stakes are high.	I soften or delay difficult truths.	I communicate honestly even when uncomfortable.	I have a practice for delivering difficult truths with care.	
Accountability modeling	I deflect or rationalize mistakes.	I acknowledge mistakes privately.	I own mistakes openly and visibly.	I model accountability so routinely it has shaped team culture.	

Consistency

Behavior	1 – Not Present	2 – Emergent	3 – Strong	4 – Systematized	Score
Behavioral predictability	I am surprised by my own reactions.	My behavior is situational.	My team can predict how I'll respond.	My responses are consistent across contexts and people.	
Standard application	Standards shift without explanation.	I apply rules unevenly.	Same standards for similar situations.	Standards are documented and applied systematically.	
Follow-through on commitments	I regularly miss commitments.	I follow through inconsistently.	I follow through reliably.	I build accountability structures that track commitments.	

Communication

Behavior	1 – Not Present	2 – Emergent	3 – Strong	4 – Systematized	Score
Transparency	Information is withheld by default.	I share some context part of the time.	I proactively communicate relevant information.	I have a structured communication cadence.	
Uncertainty communication	I stay silent when I don't have answers.	I acknowledge uncertainty occasionally.	I name uncertainty clearly and consistently.	I have a protocol for communicating under uncertainty.	
Listening quality	I listen to respond.	I listen but miss key signals.	I listen to understand.	I build feedback loops to verify understanding.	

Competence

Behavior	1 – Not Present	2 – Emergent	3 – Strong	4 – Systematized	Score
Role readiness	I'm reactive in areas I should lead.	I'm developing in key areas.	I'm capable across core responsibilities.	I'm investing in continuous growth systematically.	
System-building	I operate on instinct.	I have informal processes.	I have documented processes.	I have scalable systems that others can run.	
Delegating effectively	I hold on to work I should delegate.	I delegate inconsistently.	I delegate well with clear expectations.	I have a structured delegation handoff process.	

Care

Behavior	1 – Not Present	2 – Emergent	3 – Strong	4 – Systematized	Score
Individual awareness	I don't know what my people are carrying.	I notice some team members' needs.	I actively attend to individual well-being.	I have a structured check-in practice for every team member.	
Capacity protection	I optimize output regardless of cost.	I notice overload after it happens.	I proactively manage capacity.	I have a workload system with early-warning signals.	
Investment in growth	I don't invest in people's development.	I support development reactively.	I actively invest in each person's growth.	I have individualized development plans for every team member.	

Clarity

Behavior	1 – Not Present	2 – Emergent	3 – Strong	4 – Systematized	Score
Priority communication	My team doesn't know what matters most.	Priorities shift without explanation.	Priorities are clear and consistently communicated.	I have a structured priority communication system.	
Role and expectation clarity	Roles and expectations are ambiguous.	Some expectations are clear.	Expectations are documented and understood.	Clarity reviews happen regularly and are tracked.	
Decision transparency	Decisions happen invisibly.	I explain some decisions.	I explain the what and why of key decisions.	I have a framework for decision communication.	

Courage

Behavior	1 – Not Present	2 – Emergent	3 – Strong	4 – Systematized	Score
Difficult conversations	I consistently avoid necessary conversations.	I have them when forced.	I initiate difficult conversations proactively.	I have a practice that makes courageous conversations routine.	
Standard enforcement	I let standards slide under pressure.	I enforce standards inconsistently.	I enforce standards even when uncomfortable.	Standards are enforced through systems, not just willpower.	
Unpopular decisions	I avoid decisions that will be unpopular.	I delay necessary decisions.	I make values-based decisions despite opposition.	I communicate the "why" behind hard decisions clearly and early.	

Part 2: Pillar Score Summary

Transfer your scores from Part 1. Total each pillar (3 behaviors × max 4 = 12 per pillar). Use the interpretation guide below to identify priority actions.

Pillar	Score (1–4 per behavior)	Pillar Total (/12)	Priority Action
Character			
Consistency			
Communication			
Competence			
Care			
Clarity			
Courage			

Score Interpretation

Pillar Total	Signal	Recommended Action
3-5	Critical gap	Begin repair work. This pillar is actively eroding trust.
6–8	Emergent	Prioritize in your 90-Day Trust Build™. Improvement is needed within 30 days.
9–10	Strong	Maintain and document. Look for ways to systematize further.
11-12	Systematized	Use as a model. Consider how to leverage this pillar to support weaker ones.

Part 3: Reflection Questions

These questions are designed to move beyond the numbers. Use them after scoring, alone, in a coaching session, or in a leadership team review.

The honest look

Which pillar score surprised you most, and why? What does that gap tell you about your blind spots?

The team view

If your team scored you on this same assessment, where would their scores differ from yours? What would they see that you're not scoring accurately?

The cost

What is the organizational cost of your lowest-scoring pillar right now, in culture, in retention, or in execution quality?

The first move

If you addressed only one pillar in the next 30 days, which one would create the most leverage for everything else?

The long game

Which pillar, if systematized over the next 12 months, would most change what you're able to build?

Part 4: Scoring Cadence

A one-time assessment is a snapshot. The value of the Trust Scorecard™ compounds when used on a regular cadence. The following schedule is recommended.

Cadence	What to Assess	Focus
Weekly	Lowest-scoring pillar only	Track movement on your priority repairs. Is the behavior changing?
Monthly	All 7 pillars	Full re-score. Look for drift in pillars that were stable last month.
Quarterly	Full scorecard + reflection questions	Identify trend patterns. Are repairs holding? Where is drift returning?
Annually	Full scorecard + team comparison	Compare your self-assessment with peer or team input. Where are the largest gaps?

Appendix D

Trust Under Pressure

Note on these case studies: These are composite cases drawn from multiple leadership coaching engagements. Names, industries, and identifying details have been changed or removed. The behaviors, decisions, and outcomes reflect patterns observed across real organizations.

Scenario A: Director Mariel Chen

Rebuilding Trust After Inherited Leadership Failure

The Situation

A senior leader, let's call her Director Mariel Chen, stepped into a divisional leadership role mid-year, inheriting a team of 840 people, five direct reports, and a culture that had been destabilized by 18 months of poor leadership before her arrival.

The previous director had been inconsistent and withholding communication. The team had stopped raising problems early. They had developed informal workarounds to get things done, bypassing official channels, solving problems laterally, and keeping the director out of loops that should have included her.

By the time Mariel arrived, trust was not merely low. It was absent in three of its most structurally damaging forms: trust in leadership's competence, trust in leadership's character, and trust in leadership's willingness to be honest.

She had 90 days to stabilize the system before a major organizational review. The pressure was immediate.

Pillar	Inherited State	Priority	Key Signal
Character	Critical	1	Public statements and private behavior misaligned
Consistency	Critical	1	Standards changed by mood, not principle
Communication	Critical	1	Information withheld routinely as control
Competence	At Risk	2	Technical credibility low; systems nonexistent
Care	Critical	1	High performers left; underperformers were never held to standard
Clarity	At Risk	2	Priorities shifted without explanation or pattern
Courage	Absent	3	Avoidance was the operating norm; accountability did not exist.

What Mariel Did: The First 30 Days

Mariel's first instinct was to present a vision. She had a clear, well-developed, and compelling vision. She decided to put it on hold.

In a low-trust environment, vision lands as noise. Before a team will follow a direction, they need evidence that the person pointing is trustworthy. That evidence comes from behavior, not from vision decks.

Her first 30 days were built around three moves.

Move 1: Name What She Was Seeing

In her first all-hands meeting, Mariel did not present her vision, her bio, or her leadership philosophy. She said this:

> "I've spent my first two weeks listening to each of you, to the data, and to the patterns in how decisions have been made here. What I'm seeing is a team with real capability that has learned, reasonably, not to trust leadership.
>
> I'm not asking you to trust me. I haven't earned it yet. I'm asking you to watch.
>
> Over the next 30 days, I'll be making three commitments. I'm going to state them publicly, and I'm going to report back on them in 30 days, whether I kept them or not. That's how we start."

> **Character** Mariel chose to name the inherited trust breakdown directly rather than cover it with optimism. This is a Character move: naming the real state before asserting direction.

Move 2: Establish Visible Behavioral Standards

Her three public commitments were specific, behavioral, and observable:

1. Every week, she would hold a 20-30-minute team brief, same day, same format, and same structure. No cancellations without a 24-hour notice and a makeup schedule.

2. Every decision that affected the team would include an explanation of the reasoning, delivered within 24 hours.

3. Any performance concern she was managing privately would be surfaced to the relevant person within 72 hours of her identifying it.

> **Consistency** Notice that these commitments were chosen because they were specific and verifiable, not because they were impressive. The team could track them. That visibility is the point.

Move 3: Surface the Workarounds

In her one-on-ones during the first two weeks, Mariel asked each person the same question: "What are you solving around me that should come to me?"

Most leaders never ask this. The answers were instructive and sobering. She found four informal systems that had developed to compensate for the previous director's absence. She did not shut them down. She acknowledged them, asked what was working about them, and built formal replacements that preserved the function while restoring appropriate accountability.

> **Clarity + Care** Surfacing workarounds require both Clarity (naming the actual state of operations) and Care (treating informal systems as evidence of team intelligence, not insubordination).

Days 31–60: Testing the System

On Day 30, Mariel held a brief public review of her three commitments.

She had kept two perfectly. The third, the 72-hour feedback commitment, she had breached once, when a performance concern had slipped to Day 5 before she addressed it. She reported that publicly.

"I committed to surfacing performance concerns within 72 hours. I kept that commitment in every case except one, where I waited five days. That was a breach of what I said, and I want to name it.

Here's what I'm doing to prevent that from recurring: I've added a weekly review to my calendar, every Friday at noon, to audit whether I've held the 72-hour standard. That review is on my calendar, and anyone on this team can ask me about it."

> **Character + Courage** Naming the breach publicly, rather than hoping no one noticed, was the single most trust-building moment of Mariel's first 60 days. In a low-trust environment, visible accountability creates more credibility than consistent perfection.

By Day 45, the informal workarounds had largely dissolved. People were bringing problems to Mariel's team brief rather than solving them around her. One of her three direct reports, who had been the most skeptical, started sending her early-warning notes about operational concerns. It was the first proactive communication she had received from him.

He told her later: "I needed to see if you'd actually call yourself out. When you did, I decided you were worth trusting."

Days 61–90: Scaling the System

By Day 60, the trust infrastructure was stable enough to introduce the vision she had built in Month 1. She had earned the right to cast it.

She also began addressing the performance gaps that had been the most politically charged, two team members who had been informally protected by the previous director but were underperforming at high cost to their peers.

She used the Competence Gap framework from Appendix A, named the gap specifically, separated it from character and effort, offered a clear path, and set a timeline. Both conversations happened within the same week.

> **Courage -** Mariel had waited until Day 60 to address these gaps, not because she was avoiding them, but because she had spent the first 60 days building the credibility needed to have them land as care rather than as a threat. Timing is part of the courageous conversation.

The Rebuild Timeline

Timefram e	Pillar	Leadership Action	Observed Result
Week 1–2	Character	Named inherited trust breakdown without blame	Team is cautious but attentive
Week 1–2	Care	Asked every team member: "What are you solving around me?"	Surfaced 3 informal workarounds
Week 3–4	Consistency	Held all 4 team briefs on schedule. No cancellations.	Attendance became consistent without reminders.
Week 4	Character	Publicly reviewed three commitments. Named the breach.	Visible uptick in team engagement
Week 5–6	Communication	Introduced structured weekly brief with standard format	Questions began surfacing that were previously hidden
Week 6–7	Clarity	Documented 3 organizational priorities. Posted publicly.	Informal priority confusion began to resolve
Week 8-9	Consistency	Formalized workaround replacements. Acknowledged team intelligence.	Trust in the process began to build
Week 10	Courage	Addressed two performance gaps that had been politically avoided	Team morale improved; fairness signal restored

What Changed—and What Didn't

By Day 90, the divisional trust score (measured through a structured team feedback process) had improved across all seven pillars. The gains were not evenly distributed.

Character, Consistency, and Communication showed the sharpest improvement because these were the areas Mariel had targeted first and most visibly. Competence and Courage showed meaningful but slower progress. The systems weren't fully built yet. The performance conversations were recent. These would take longer to compound.

What didn't change: the organizational review was still difficult. Several structural challenges remained unresolved. Two team members who had been most damaged by the previous director's behavior chose to leave during the 90 days, not because of Mariel, but because the trust damage ran too deep to recover within the timeframe they were willing to invest.

Mariel called that an acceptable outcome. "I couldn't repair 18 months of damage in 90 days. What I could do was make the culture worth staying in for the people who were still willing to try."

Key Lessons

Pillar	Lesson
Character	Name the real state before asserting direction. Vision without credibility is noise.
Consistency	Public commitments are only powerful if you track and report on them. The tracking is the trust-builder.
Communication	In a low-trust environment, acknowledging the absence of trust is more effective than projecting confidence.
Competence	System-building during active repair signals that the leader is thinking past the crisis. That signal matters.
Care	Informal workarounds are evidence of team intelligence, not resistance. Ask about them. Build formal replacements that honor what they were solving.
Clarity	Public accountability requires documented standards. You cannot hold yourself to something you haven't named.
Courage	Some performance conversations require an earned foundation before they can land. Timing is a leadership decision, not avoidance.

Discussion Questions

Use the following questions for personal reflection, coaching sessions, or leadership team discussions.

The inherited state

How do you take ownership of trust gaps you didn't create? What is the difference between taking responsibility and taking blame?

The vision decision

Mariel delayed presenting her vision for 60 days. Under what conditions is delaying a vision the right move? When does delay become avoidance?

The breach naming

Naming a public breach of commitment is one of the highest-risk and highest-reward trust moves a leader can make. What makes it so rare? What stops leaders from doing it?

The timeline

Mariel addressed the performance gaps at Day 60 rather than Day 5. Was this courageous or strategic? Can those two things be the same?

Your own version

Where in your current leadership context is there a trust gap you've inherited? What would the equivalent of Mariel's first 30 days look like in your situation?

Scenario B: Superintendent David Reyes

Navigating a $3.2 Million State Budget Cut While Building Trust

Composite Case Study: This case is drawn from patterns common across superintendencies navigating externally imposed fiscal stress. Names, districts, and specific details have been changed or removed. The trust dynamics, decision frameworks, and leadership responses reflect real challenges that education leaders face.

Overview

In his third year leading Andover Public School District, Superintendent David Reyes received devastating news from the state capitol. The governor's office announced mid-year that a state revenue shortfall had forced an across-the-board reduction in education funding. For Andover, the math was swift and precise: a $3.2 million cut to state aid, effective in the current fiscal year, with the possibility of further reductions in the cycle ahead.

The district had done nothing wrong. It had not overspent. It had not made reckless commitments. It had, in fact, just completed the first year of a thoughtful, community-supported, five-year strategic plan, built on prudent assumptions and board-approved priorities. Now, through no fault of its own, Andover was facing a structural hole that would require real decisions about what to preserve, what to reduce, and how to tell the truth about both.

What made the situation particularly layered was context. Two of the strategic plan's cornerstone commitments, expanding mental health supports and deepening early literacy interventions, were starting to show results. The community had rallied around the plan. The board had approved it unanimously. And now, before momentum could fully build, Reyes had to stand before those same stakeholders and explain that the financial ground had shifted, not because of poor leadership, but because the state had cut the floor out from under districts across the region.

The trust question wasn't abstract. It was immediate: Would Andover's board, staff, families, and community believe that Reyes and his cabinet could protect what mattered most while making hard choices responsibly, even when the crisis wasn't their fault?

The Trust Challenge

Trust Pillar	Specific Challenge in This Scenario
Character	When the crisis wasn't your fault, the temptation is to lead with the blame. How do you demonstrate that your values, not just your competence, are guiding the response? How do you show staff and community that you're making the right call, not just the safe one?
Consistency	The strategic plan made promises. The state changed the math. How do you honor the spirit of commitment even when resources have been taken away?
Communication	How do you structure communication to a board, staff, families, and community simultaneously, with each needing the truth but in different forms? How do you keep people informed without getting ahead of decisions not yet made?
Competence	The board and community need to see that the cabinet analyzed this thoroughly, acted quickly, and protected the most essential work first.
Care	Families will ask, "Are you cutting programs my child depends on?" The staff will ask, "Is my position safe?" Both questions require honest, human answers.
Clarity	How do you explain a $3.2M state-driven cut without sounding like you're passing the blame? How do you maintain integrity without creating panic?
Courage	Some decisions will disappoint people: staff, families, and community members. Reyes has to make them anyway and own them publicly.

Situation Snapshot

District profile: Mid-sized suburban district, 7,200 students, 11 schools, 780 staff

Deficit: $3.2 million driven by a mid-year state budget shortfall and corresponding reduction in state aid to local education agencies.

Strategic plan commitments at stake: Mental health expansion (three social workers and one school psychologist hired in Year 1); early literacy intervention staffing; instructional coaching model; community partnership programming.

Political/community context: The board had approved the strategic plan unanimously. A parent advocacy group had organized specifically around the mental health expansion. A vocal minority had opposed the strategic plan from the outset.

What Reyes and his Cabinet Did: 30/60/90 Day Response

Days 1–30: Honest Assessment Before Public Communication

Before any board meeting, public statement, or community forum, Reyes required his cabinet to complete a full financial analysis, not to spin a narrative, but to understand what was actually true. He was explicit with his team: We are not going to present options we haven't fully vetted. We are not going to promise what we can't deliver. And we are not going to let the state's decision become an excuse for our own lack of discipline.

Cabinet actions in the first 30 days:

- Confirmed the $3.2M reduction figure directly with the state department of education.
- Identified and categorized all expenditures by classification: instructional, operational, administrative, and strategic plan commitments.
- Directed all cabinet members to cut non-personnel operating budgets by 10% immediately, no exceptions, generating approximately $710,000 in Year 1.

- Committed to an additional 5% non-personnel reduction in the following budget cycle, signaling structural discipline rather than one-time fixes.
- Launched a comprehensive review of all software and technology contracts district-wide, the initial scan identified 14 contracts totaling $280,000 in potential renegotiation or cancellation candidates.
- Developed three budget scenarios, conservative, moderate, and strategic preservation, each with an honest tradeoff analysis.

Days 31–60: Board Engagement and Transparent Communication

Reyes requested a special study session with the full board before the issue appeared on any public agenda. He brought his full cabinet, his auditor, and a complete financial presentation, including how the state cut had impacted the district, what the district had already done in the first 30 days, and what decisions remained.

He named the problem clearly:

> "The state has reduced our funding by $3.2 million. This is not a cash flow issue, not a one-year anomaly we can paper over; it is a structural change to our revenue base that requires structural decisions on our part."

He acknowledged the irony without using it as cover: the mental health staff hired under the strategic plan, three social workers and a school psychologist, represented the kind of investment the community had asked for. Protecting them meant other things would have to be reduced.

He presented the cabinet's own discipline first: the 10% non-personnel cuts, the planned second-cycle reduction, and the software contract review. He offered three paths, with honest consequences for each. No path was presented as painless.

When a board member asked, "How is it fair that we're punished for a state decision we had nothing to do with?" Reyes answered directly:

> "It isn't fair, and I won't pretend otherwise. But fairness doesn't change our obligation to the children in our schools. What we control is how we respond, and that is what I intend to get right."

Days 61–90: Community Engagement and the Path Forward

Reyes held four community listening sessions across the district in seven days, including evening sessions for working families and a Spanish-language session with interpretation. He brought his cabinet to every one.

The sessions were not comfortable. Parents asked hard questions. The staff were anxious. The faction that had opposed the strategic plan showed up arguing the plan itself had caused the district's financial problems, a claim that was factually false but emotionally resonant.

Reyes held a consistent framework in every session:

- Here is what happened at the state level and what it means for Andover.
- Here is what we have already done before coming to you.
- Here is what we are recommending and why.
- Here is what we will protect, and here is what will change.
- Here is how you can stay informed and engaged.

By day 87, the board had unanimously approved a budget reduction plan that included position reductions through attrition (not layoffs), preservation of all strategic plan mental health staff, consolidation of two administrative positions, and a software contract reduction of $280,000 from the contract review. Additionally, the board voted to use their rainy day fund to cover the remaining cuts and committed to rebuilding their structural reserves back over three years.

Trust Rebuild Timeline

Phase	Timeline	Trust Signal	Outcome
Internal discipline	Days 1–30	10% non-personnel cuts; software contract review launched	Cabinet credibility established; board sees action, not just reaction
Transparent board engagement	Days 31–45	Full presentation, three scenarios, no spin	Board trust restored; members feel respected and informed
Community listening	Days 46–75	Five sessions, multilingual, cabinet present	Families feel heard even when they disagree with decisions
Budget adoption	Day 87	Unanimous board vote	Institutional confidence restored; strategic plan survives
Year 2 follow-through	Months 4–12	2nd-cycle cuts enacted; $280K software savings realized	Competence validated; commitments honored

The Mental Health Question: A Trust Test Within the Test

The mental health expansion deserves specific attention because it became the most emotionally charged element of the community conversation. When Andover families learned of the state cut, many assumed the three social workers and school psychologist were at risk. The parent advocacy group had organized specifically around these positions. Community trust in those roles, and in Reyes, was fragile.

Reyes made a deliberate choice: he named the mental health staff specifically, in every public setting, as protected. Not as a political calculation, but because it was the right call. The students those staff members served, children navigating anxiety, family trauma, and post-pandemic social disruption, were among the district's most vulnerable. Cutting them to balance a budget built on non-essential operating costs would have been a false economy and a moral failure.

He told the community plainly:

"The state cut our funding. That is real, and it requires real decisions, but it does not change the fact that our students need mental health support. Three social workers and a school psychologist are now part of the fabric of our schools. We hired them because it was right, and we are keeping them because it is still right."

That statement, repeated consistently, became one of the defining trust anchors of the entire budget process.

Key Lessons

Lesson	Application
External causes do not eliminate internal accountability.	The state created the problem. Reyes still owned the response. Leaders who spend energy on blame, even justified blame, lose time and credibility they cannot recover.
Visible discipline earns the right to ask others to absorb pain.	The 10% non-personnel cuts and software contract review were not just savings measures; they were trust signals. Leaders who cut themselves last lose credibility.
Name what you're protecting and why.	Abstract budget language erodes trust. Specific commitments, naming the mental health staff and the literacy positions, restored it.
Unanimous board votes are earned, not given.	Three board members had publicly championed the strategic plan. Reyes brought them into the process early. They voted yes because they trusted the process.
Community tension, handled with integrity, can become community cohesion.	The faction that blamed the strategic plan showed up at community sessions. Reyes engaged them respectfully and with facts. Several became less adversarial.
A strategic plan is not a liability in a crisis; it is a compass.	Because the plan existed, Reyes had a clear framework for what to protect. Without it, every budget decision would have been arbitrary.

Trust Framework Reflection

All seven pillars were engaged in this case, but Competence and Courage were the load-bearing ones.

> **Competence** The board and community needed to know that the cabinet had analyzed the state cuts rigorously and responded quickly with discipline. The 5% non-personnel cuts, the software contract review, and the three-scenario board presentation were not communication strategies. They were evidence of a cabinet that knew what it was doing even when the ground shifted beneath them.
>
> **Courage** Reyes had to stand in rooms full of anxious people and say hard things clearly, including pushing back on the false narrative that the strategic plan had caused the problem. He could not soften the cut into non-existence. He could only commit to integrity throughout the process, and he did.

Discussion Questions

1. Reyes chose not to lead public communication with "the state did this to us," even though that was factually accurate. Do you agree with that choice? How do you distinguish between honest context and deflection?

2. The cabinet's decision to immediately cut non-personnel budgets by 10% was described as a "trust signal" as much as a fiscal measure. What signals are you currently sending, or not sending, that shape how your staff and community perceive your fiscal stewardship?

3. Reyes explicitly protected the mental health staff despite the state cut. When you face externally imposed resource constraints, how do you decide what is protected and what is reduced? What framework guides that decision?

4. Some neighboring districts responded to the same state cut with immediate program eliminations. How do you hold to a principled response when peer districts are making different choices and community members notice?

5. The software contract review generated $280,000 in savings. Where in your organization are there commitments, contracts, or expenditures that have never been examined because they predate your tenure or feel too complicated to touch?

6. If you were Reyes on the day the state announcement came, before any analysis was complete, what would you have done first? What would have been your biggest temptation to avoid?

A Final Ask

If something in these pages reframed how you think about trust, gave language to a conversation you have been avoiding, or helped you recognize a pattern in your own leadership, I would ask one thing of you.

Please take ninety seconds to leave an honest review on Amazon.

Reviews help other leaders discover this work. They also help me understand what is resonating in real leadership environments, and what still needs sharpening.

Your honest perspective matters far more than a perfect rating.

Scan the QR code below to leave your review.

Thank you for reading. Thank you for leading.

— Gearl Loden

About the Author

Gearl Loden, Ph.D., MBA, is the Founder and CEO of Loden Leadership and Consulting Group and the architect of the Loden Trust Framework™. His work centers on the discipline of trust as leadership infrastructure, the operating system behind durable performance, culture, and decision-making.

He coaches CEOs, founders, nonprofit and educational leaders, and high-capacity professionals operating under significant decision pressure. His proprietary four-step Loden Trust Method™ (Diagnose, Repair, Build, Protect) is the same system used inside private executive engagements with senior leaders across business, education, and the nonprofit sector.

A 2025 NASS National Superintendent of the Year Finalist, a 2015 Mississippi Superintendent of the Year, and a recognized National Influencer of the Year for his work in district turnaround and leadership development, he writes from inside the chair, not above it.

His insights on leadership, trust, and executive performance have been featured in *Fast Company, Authority Magazine, Buffalo News, Grit Daily, Under30CEO, High Net Worth Magazine,* and more than sixty additional leadership and business publications.

The deepest applications of the framework take place inside private engagements with his firm: executive coaching, board strategy and trust reviews, leadership transition planning, and keynote speaking and leadership intensives.

To inquire about coaching, speaking, or advisory work, visit lodenleadership.com.

Lighting the Path.

Connect with the Author

Before It Breaks was written to be used, not just read. If this framework has shaped how you think about trust in your organization, Gearl would like to hear from you.

Coaching & Consulting

Gearl works with senior leaders, executive teams, and superintendents on trust-based leadership, organizational culture, and high-stakes change. Engagements include one-on-one executive coaching, leadership team intensives, and district or organizational consulting.

Speaking

Gearl is available for keynotes, leadership conferences, superintendent gatherings, and corporate events. His presentations are built on the Loden Trust Framework™ and designed to move audiences from insight to immediate application.

The Hopewell Project

In partnership with his wife, Monica Loden, PMHNP, the Hopewell Project supports leaders navigating mental health challenges in their organizations and their own lives. Learn more at lodenleadership.com.

Master Classes

Loden Leadership offers master classes for leaders and coaches who want to go deeper into the seven pillars, the diagnostic tools, and the trust-repair protocols in this book.

The Companion Workbook

Before It Breaks: The Complete Leadership Workbook — The Seven Pillars of TRUST Every Leader Must Build is available wherever books are sold.

Visit: lodenleadership.com

Email: gearlloden@lodenleadership.com

Phone: 1-877-619-GROW (4769)

BEFORE IT BREAKS: RESOURCES

YOUR PURCHASE INCLUDES FREE RESOURCES

Thank you for investing in *Before It Breaks*. Your copy includes access to a free Reader Resource Bundle, built to help you move from insight to action.

To claim your resources, register your purchase at masterclass.lodenleadership.com/resource.

Or scan the QR code on this page.

Your resource download code is TRUST7

Your bundle includes:

The Before It Breaks Template Bundle: Your complete set of 11 fillable leadership tools built directly from the book and the Loden Trust Framework™. Available in fillable digital and clean print versions. Your tools include:

- The Trust Audit™
- The Leadership Ledger™
- The Trust Signal Dashboard™
- The 72-Hour Repair Protocol™
- The 90-Day Trust Build™
- The Trust Conversation Framework™
- Advanced Trust Diagnostics
- The Trust Scorecard™
- The Capability-Commitment Diagnostic™
- The Drip Decision Protocol™
- The Trust-Protection Sequence™

Free Before It Breaks Masterclass Access: As a verified book buyer, you are invited to join an exclusive live masterclass with Dr. Loden. This 60-minute session unpacks select components of the Loden Trust Framework™ with real-world application, followed by a live Q&A. Cohorts are limited and offered exclusively to verified book readers.

Mastermind Waitlist Priority Access: First-in-line consideration for the next cohort of the Before It Breaks Mastermind, reserved exclusively for verified book readers.

Growth Alliance Membership: Join Dr. Loden's leadership community for ongoing insights, live Q&As, and peer connection with purpose-driven leaders nationwide.

The 7 Pillars Quick Reference Card: A single-page PDF listing each pillar, its core definition, and one diagnostic question for immediate application.

The Trust Vocabulary Glossary: A comprehensive reference guide to key terms and phrases from the book for easy reference and team sharing.

Registration is free. Your resources will be delivered immediately upon confirmation.

For leaders ready to go deeper, visit lodenleadership.com to explore coaching and mastermind opportunities.

"Trust is not built in a moment. It is built in every moment that matters."
— Gearl Loden, Ph.D.

lodenleadership.com | #BeforeItBreaks | #LodenLeadership

www.ingramcontent.com/pod-product-compliance
Lightning Source LLC
LaVergne TN
LVHW091254150826
845673LV00006B/1415

9798995217718